OUT
OF THE

A DAILY DEVOTIONAL FROM
THE BOOK OF MATTHEW

© 2025 by Elle-Louise James. All rights reserved. No part of this publication may be reproduced, distributed, or transmitted in any form or by any means, including photocopying, recording, or other electronic or mechanical methods, without the prior written permission of the publisher, except in the case of brief quotations embodied in critical reviews and certain other noncommercial uses permitted by copyright law. For permission requests, write to the publisher at *jamesellelouise@gmail.com*

Bible References:
All Scripture quotations are taken from the New King James Version® (NKJV), © 1982 by Thomas Nelson, Inc. Used by permission. All rights reserved.

New King James Version (NKJV) Bible References:
For all scripture references in this devotional, the verses have been taken from the New King James Version (NKJV). The NKJV is a modern translation first published in 1982 by Thomas Nelson, preserving the beauty and accuracy of the King James Version while updating the language to make it more accessible to contemporary readers. It maintains the poetic structure and faithfulness to the original texts while providing clarity for modern understanding.

New Living Translation (NLT) Bible References:
All scripture references from the Bible in this devotional are taken from the New Living Translation (NLT). The NLT was first published in 1996 by Tyndale House Publishers and is a modern translation that seeks to make the biblical text more accessible and understandable in contemporary English. The translation is based on the most recent scholarship in translation and biblical studies. Used by permission, all rights reserved.

Dedication

To my Good Father, God.
And Jesus came and spoke to them, saying:
"All authority in heaven and on earth has been given to Me. Go, therefore, and make disciples of all nations, baptizing them in the name of the Father, the Son, and the Holy Spirit, teaching them to observe everything I have commanded you. And surely, I am with you always, to the very end of the age."
— Matthew 28:18-20

Contents

Introduction 1

Reading 1. Origin Stories 6
Reading 2. Fearful but Obedient 10
Reading 3. Insecure 14
Reading 4. Purpose Protected 18
Reading 5. Right Repentance 22
Reading 6. Humility in the Wilderness 26
Reading 7. Fighting Temptations 30
Reading 8. Silent Endings 34
Reading 9. Immediate Response 38
Reading 10. The Comfort of the King 42
Reading 11. A Different Kind of Bright 46
Reading 12. True Righteousness 50
Reading 13. Murder in the Heart 54
Reading 14. Safeguarding Purity 58
Reading 15. Preparing for a Lifelong Love 62
Reading 16. Our Word Should Be Enough 66
Reading 17. The Extra Mile 70
Reading 18. Private Givers 74
Reading 19. The Covenant of Prayer 78
Reading 20. Where is Your Treasure? 82
Reading 21. The Antidote to Worry 86

Reading 22. Beyond Appearances 90
Reading 23. The Power of Submission. 94
Reading 24. The Battle We Cannot See 98
Reading 25. Making Room for the New 102
Reading 26. Valued and Seen 106
Reading 27. How Will You Be Described? 110
Reading 28. The Cost of Discipleship:
            What Do You Love Most? 114
Reading 29. A Lighter Load 118
Reading 30. Rule Keepers with Rigid Hearts 122
Reading 31. Understanding Blasphemy 126
Reading 32. The Ongoing Journey of the Heart. 130
Reading 33. When Familiarity Breeds Contempt 134
Reading 34. More than a Beheading 138
Reading 35. Sent into the Storm. 142
Reading 36. The Heart of the Matter 146
Reading 37. Persistent Faith and Humility 150
Reading 38. Remembering God's Faithfulness. 154
Reading 39. Testing the Teachings. 158
Reading 40. On Guard. 162
Reading 41. Will You Follow? 166
Reading 42. Warfare in the Spiritual Realm 170
Reading 43. From Status to Servanthood 174
Reading 44. Chasing the One 178
Reading 45. Privacy First. 182
Reading 46. The Infinite Call to Forgiveness 186
Reading 47. Bringing the Next Generation to Jesus 190
Reading 48. An Invitation to True Freedom. 194

Reading 49. The Power of Context 198
Reading 50. Kingdom Culture: A Reversal. 202
Reading 51. A Generous God. 206
Reading 52. Specificity. 210
Reading 53. Fickle Follower or Faithful Disciple? 214
Reading 54. Handling Difficult People 218
Reading 55. The Chosen 222
Reading 56. The Love Triangle. 226
Reading 57. A Call to Self-Examination 230
Reading 58. Suffering Well 234
Reading 59. A Sense of Urgency. 238
Reading 60. Does Your Faith Have a Price? 242
Reading 61. Grace Beyond Failure. 246
Reading 62. The Wrestle 250
Reading 63. The Kiss of Betrayal 254
Reading 64. Purity on Trial. 258
Reading 65. People Watchers 262
Reading 66. The Cost. 266
Reading 67. Silence is Never Neutral. 270
Reading 68. The Crucifixion. 274
Reading 69. God of the Detail 278
Reading 70. Our Great Commission. 282

Epilogue 287
Acknowledgments 289

Introduction

I never set out to write a book, and definitely not a devotional. The few I'd read seemed to lead me towards deeper waters, only to stop short at the water's edge. Hence the title, *Out of the Shallows*. I never could find a devotional that pushed me to wade beyond the shoreline and really submerge myself in my reading for that day. So, what to do? As Toni Morrison once said: "If there's a book that you want to read, but it hasn't been written yet, then you must write it."

My hope is that the reflection questions and tasks at the end of each reading will take you beyond the shallows to achieve three things.

First, I hope they make you stop and think. In today's culture, it's easy to scroll the Internet and find all kinds of pre-packaged beliefs. However, what we really need is less content and more time to reflect on God's Word, which is "living and powerful" (Hebrews 4:12). When we read the Bible, it should challenge us, provoke thought, and inspire questioning. Don't just accept my interpretations as you read these pages – instead, ask questions and push back, even if I'm not there to converse with you. Be active.

This leads to the second aim of this book, which is to inspire you to read more. **To this day,** the Bible remains the most purchased book – yes, even in our secular society. Yet, I sometimes wonder how well read it is. I want to inspire you not just to read God's Word, but to dive deeper – to explore the cultural context of the verses, their historical and religious backdrop, and the nuances of the time when Matthew was writing.

Finally, the last goal of this book is the most important. It's to draw you closer to God. Ultimately, a book about God should draw us closer to Him. This is my prayer for everyone who reads this devotional.

The body of the devotional will focus on the Book of Matthew, a Gospel that is traditionally attributed to one of Jesus' twelve disciples, Matthew, who was a Jew and tax collector. As you read, it will help to recall that Matthew's primary audience was Jewish. It will also help to be aware that Matthew's status as a tax collector would have made him despised amongst the Jewish people, who were already oppressed by Roman rule. If you've ever felt marginalised or isolated due to your choices, Matthew would have fully understood your experience. Yet, Jesus saw something in Matthew – as He does in all of us – and asked Matthew to follow Him.

As the first book in the New Testament, the Book of Matthew bridges the Old and the New Testament. It connects the prophecies and promises of the Old Testament with their fulfilment in Jesus Christ.

How should you read this book?

Out of the Shallows contains 70 readings. It is designed as a daily devotional, with each reading following from the previous chapter or verse in the Gospel. A sequential approach will take you step by step through each of Matthew's 28 chapters, from the genealogy of Jesus all the way through to the Great Commission. This is the best method to use if you wish to ground yourself in the overarching story and wisdom of this Gospel.

However, you can also explore the readings out of sequential order, based on the themes and questions that are most pertinent to your day ahead or current struggles. There is perennial strength and solace to be found in these verses no matter what you are facing in life; I therefore encourage you to peruse these pages, and return to them beyond your initial study, to seek out the wisdom you need in the moment.

As for the version of the Bible used, all the Bible verses referenced are taken from either the New King James version or the New Living Translation. However, I recommend that you read the text for each devotional using whatever version helps you best understand the words and message.

With that, this devotional begins with the first chapter of Matthew. From there, it will prompt you to draw out wisdom and insights that you can apply to your Christian Walk. May the questions and tasks ahead guide you out of the shallows and into the deepness of God's grace.

Elle Louise James
February 2025

OUT
OF THE
Shallows

Origin Stories

"Every man is a quotation from all his ancestors." - Ralph Waldo Emerson

1. Reading: Matthew 1:1-17

*I*n any story, beginnings matter. Books and films rarely start at the end. Instead, they carefully weave together the characters' backstories because beginnings provide context. Our culture has become obsessed with tracing ancestry. As Christians, we have three sources that shape our identity. Firstly, we are created in the *imago Dei*, the image of God; this is our most authentic identity. Secondly, we descend from our ancestors Adam and Eve who passed down their sinful nature to us (Romans 5:12). Thirdly, we are born into the biological family that provides us with our identity and sense of self.

It is tempting to skip over the first half of Matthew 1 and dismiss it as a rambling list of hard-to-pronounce names. Yet in Jesus' genealogy, we see the psychological genius of God. He closes the gap between us no matter the family we come from. Among Jesus' ancestors, we find Abraham, a liar; Jacob (the grandson), also a liar and con artist; Rahab, a reformed prostitute; Boaz, every single woman's ideal man; and David, an adulterer and murderer. Through the human failures and triumphs in Jesus' ancestry, God shows us that our family of origin does not define our identity or purpose. None of us can control the family we are born into. Some of us have had wonderful families, some come from broken homes, some of us have had parents who died and were unable to raise us, and, sadly, some have been raised in care because our parents neglected us. Whatever our origin story, as Christians, we have two superseding truths. Firstly, God is our ultimate Father, ever-present and loving. Secondly, whatever our origin, our most authentic identity arises from God. His purpose for us should be what shapes the trajectory of our lives.

Reflections

How has your origin story, with its blessings and challenges, shaped your relationship with God? In what ways can you embrace both the good and the challenging aspects of your story to deepen your faith?

Considering your origin story, how has your understanding of God's purpose for your life evolved over time? What steps can you take to align yourself more closely with His purpose?

Consider a part of your origin story that has caused you pain. How might God be inviting you to find healing in this area, and how can your journey of healing serve as a testimony to others?

....
....
....
....
....
....
....
....

Fearful but Obedient

"Faith is taking the first step
even when you don't see the
whole staircase."
- Martin Luther King Jr.

2. Reading: Matthew 1:18-25

Joseph is an unsung hero in the story of Jesus' birth. If we read too hastily, we may fail to grasp the real heartache that Joseph must have felt when he learnt Mary was pregnant, knowing he wasn't the father. His betrothal to Mary legally made her his wife in Jewish culture. The only way to dissolve the relationship would have been through divorce or death. However, though Joseph was not Jesus' biological father, his obedience provided physical and spiritual shelter for Mary and Jesus.

God sent an angel to ask Joseph to stay with Mary but first addressed Joseph's emotional pain because God cares about our emotions. The angel tells Joseph, "…do not fear to take Mary as your wife…" (Matthew 1:20). The angel then quells Joseph's fears by answering his unspoken questions, explaining how Mary became pregnant and the purpose of Jesus' birth. Joseph could have politely declined God's call and found a less complicated second wife, but easy doesn't always mean fulfilling. Had Joseph chosen a different path, he would have missed out on being part of Jesus' life.

Sometimes, God will ask us to do things that make us fearful and leave us questioning Him. Joseph's response teaches us that obedience is not the absence of fear but trusting God to be with us despite our fear. The transition into spiritual maturity comes when we understand that God is more concerned about saving us and refining our character than He is our temporary comfort.

Reflections

Can you identify an area in your life where fear is holding you back from obeying God's call? What steps can you take to overcome this fear?

Reflect on a time when you obeyed God despite not fully understanding the situation. How did that experience shape your faith?

Insecure

"Jealousy is conceived only in insecurity and must be nourished in fear."
- Maya Angelou

3. Reading: Matthew 2:1-18

At some point we have all felt insecure about something, but, as Christians, insecurity should not be our predominant experience. Entrenched insecurity robs us of joy and our trust that God has created us with value and individual purpose.

King Herod was insecure, and the prophecy of Jesus' birth sparked fear in him. Herod's insecurity led him to feel anxious (Matthew 2:3) and lie to the wise men about his true intentions, which were to have Jesus killed (Matthew 2:8,16). While Herod probably didn't intend to murder innocent babies en masse, we see in him an extreme example of what unchecked insecurity can lead someone to do.

What can we take from Herod's story? Firstly, we need to bring our insecurities to God and ask God to show us our worth. Herod's life highlights that we cannot ignore insecurity because, when left unchecked, it grows and can lead us to do things out of line with God and His will for our lives.

Secondly, Herod was king, but he could not fully enjoy his purpose because he was worried about the birth of Christ (someone else's purpose). God has a unique calling for all of us in our lives and doesn't want us to miss it, nor fail to enjoy the journey because we are comparing ourselves to and competing with others.

Thankfully, most of us will never go so far as to commit infanticide. However, Herod's story underscores the seriousness of not dealing with our insecurities.

Reflections

Identify a recurring insecurity in your life. Reflect on how this insecurity has influenced your decisions and relationships. How might recognising its origins help you break free from its grip?

Consider how your insecurities might have affected your relationships with others. Have they ever led you to act out of fear, jealousy, or a sense of comparison? What steps can you take to foster healthier, more secure connections?

....
....
....
....
....
....
....
....
....
....
....
....

Purpose Protected

"The will of God will never
take you where the grace
of God cannot protect you."
- Anonymous

4. Reading: Matthew 2:19-23

*I*n the classic British children's puzzle series *Where's Wally?* readers search for a figure who is hidden in plain sight among various distractions. This theme of hiddenness is not dissimilar to Jesus' early life, when God divinely protected Him from King Herod's murderous intent. Herod's search for Jesus was more than just a manifestation of insecurity; it was Satan's attempt to derail God's redemptive plan by eliminating Jesus before He could fulfil His divine purpose.

Jesus' mission on earth was to live a sinless life in a sinful world, demonstrating that righteousness is attainable. However, Satan, through Herod, attempted to thwart this mission by destroying Jesus while He was still a baby. God's intervention – which came first by warning the wise men and then by instructing Joseph to flee to Egypt – was crucial in safeguarding Jesus' purpose.

This passage teaches us that God's plans cannot be stopped by human or demonic interference. Just as He protected Jesus, He protects our God-given purposes, guiding us through challenges and dangers. Our role is to be obedient and trust that God is actively working to fulfil His purpose in our lives.

Reflections

Reflect on the times in your life when you felt God was guiding you towards a specific purpose. How has God protected or redirected you to ensure that you stay on the path He has laid out for you?

Joseph's obedience was crucial in protecting Jesus' life. What steps of obedience might God be calling you to take in your life right now to protect or fulfil your purpose?

How does knowing that God actively protects our purpose change your approach to challenges or fears? What practical steps can you take to lean into this truth?

....
....
....
....
....
....
....
....
....
....
....
....
....
....

Right Repentance

"Repentance is not just a feeling of sorrow; it is a decision to turn away from sin." - Charles Spurgeon

5. Reading: Matthew 3:7-12

"Brood of vipers!" John the Baptist's words to the Pharisees and Sadducees (Matthew 3:7) may seem harsh, even unloving, without context. However, John saw through their insincere hearts, prompting him to challenge them: "Produce fruit in keeping with repentance" (Matthew 3:8). John's message is as relevant now as it was then – true repentance requires more than just feeling sorry; it demands a full turning away from sin that spurs tangible, lasting change in our lives.

Repentance isn't about trying to earn forgiveness; Jesus already did that for us on the Cross. Instead, it's about responding to His grace and allowing our hearts to be transformed by the Holy Spirit. Let's consider two disciples: Peter and Judas. Both failed Jesus, but their responses couldn't have been more different.

Peter, after denying Jesus, wept bitterly in sincere repentance and went on to become a key figure in the early Church. His repentance was *metanoeō* – a heartfelt change leading to action. Judas, on the other hand, experienced regret but not true repentance. His attempt to return the 30 pieces of silver (Matthew 27:3) was driven by guilt, not a genuine turn towards God. Judas' sorrow was *metamellomai*, which means regret; it did not extend beyond feeling into action. Without true repentance there can be no change. Regret alone can only lead to despair, not redemption or transformation.

Repentance is a journey of the heart, a process of turning away from our sins and aligning our lives with God's standard, found in His Word. The grace we receive from Jesus' sacrifice on the Cross should move us to live differently, producing the fruits of true repentance in every aspect of our lives.

True repentance isn't just about what we turn away from; it's about what we turn towards.

Reflections

Reflect on a time when you felt regret but didn't fully turn away from the sin. What held you back from true repentance, and how might you approach it differently now?

Consider the difference between Peter's and Judas' responses to their failures. How does understanding their stories shape your approach to repentance?

How does the grace of God, shown through Jesus' sacrifice, motivate you to live a life of true repentance?

....
....
....
....
....
....
....

Humility in the Wilderness

"Humility is not thinking less of yourself, but thinking of yourself less."
- C.S. Lewis

6. Reading: Matthew 3:11

Humility is the practice of maintaining a balanced view and not thinking too highly nor too lowly of oneself. For some of us, God's purpose may lead to influence and success on a national or global scale. However, the key to stewarding this kind of success lies in humility.

John the Baptist is a powerful example of humility. If he were alive today, he might fill massive venues like the O2 Arena in London or Madison Square Garden in New York, even if only out of a public curiosity to see a man dressed in camel skin! His preaching attracted crowds from Jerusalem, Judea, and the Jordan Valley (Matthew 3:5). However, despite his widespread influence, John remained humble, stating, "He who is coming after me is mightier than I" (Matthew 3:11).

John's humility was rooted in two key practices: staying focused on Jesus and understanding his purpose. His focus on Jesus was evident in his message, which consistently pointed people towards the coming Messiah. This teaches us the importance of redirecting praise and success back to God, either publicly or through private prayers of gratitude.

John also understood that his purpose was to prepare the way for Christ, a task much larger than himself. Knowing our purpose keeps us humble because it reminds us that our lives and successes serve a greater plan. No matter how successful we become, our ultimate purpose is to share the message of Jesus. This is the most humbling and fulfilling mission we can undertake, and the greatest accolade we should aspire to is hearing God say, "Well done, good and faithful servant" (Matthew 25:23).

Reflections

When you receive praise or recognition, how do you typically respond? Reflect on whether you tend to internalise the praise or redirect it back to God, and why that might be.

In what ways can you keep your focus on Jesus in your daily life, especially when experiencing success? Consider practical steps like daily prayers of gratitude, sharing your faith, or involving God in your decision-making processes.

Are there areas in your life where pride might be creeping in? Think about how you can counteract pride by focusing on humility and seeking ways to serve others and glorify God.

....
....
....
....
....
....
....

Fighting Temptations

"No temptation has overtaken you except what is common to man."
- 1 Corinthians 10:13

7. Reading: Matthew 4:1-11

Most of us are familiar with Jesus' temptation in the wilderness, but there's much to unpack in this well-known passage. The Greek word used here for 'temptation' is *peirazō*, which can mean to test, examine, or tempt. In this context, it's clear that Jesus was being tested rather than tempted to sin, since we know God doesn't tempt us (James 1:13). Instead, God allows tests to strengthen us, much like He did with Adam and Eve in the Garden of Eden.

This passage offers two key strategies to help us overcome temptation.

Firstly, it's important to remember that Jesus was "led by the Spirit into the wilderness to be tempted by the devil" (Matthew 4:1). This is crucial – where God leads, He also provides and protects. Jesus wasn't set up to fail; He had everything He needed to overcome the devil's schemes. This should reassure us that if God allows us to face a test, He will equip us with the strength needed to succeed. It also highlights the importance of not willingly placing ourselves in situations where we're likely to be tempted.

Secondly, Jesus didn't rely on physical strength or weapons to overcome the devil; He relied solely on the Word of God. Every time the devil tempted Him, Jesus responded with Scripture. For example, when Satan urged Him to turn stones into bread, Jesus replied, "It is written, 'Man shall not live by bread alone, but by every word that proceeds from the mouth of God'" (Matthew 4:4). This teaches us that the most powerful weapon we have against temptation is God's Word. To overcome the enemy, we need to know Scripture and apply it directly to our situations.

Temptation and testing will be part of our lives until Jesus returns. However, we don't need to feel defeated. Jesus shows us that victory is possible – even in our fallen state. He went into the wilderness armed with the Spirit and God's Word. We should do the same.

Reflections

How well do you know Scripture that speaks directly to the temptations you face? What steps can you take to deepen your understanding and application of God's Word?

In what ways can you seek out or build a community that supports you during times of testing? How might your community help you stay grounded in God's Word?

....
....
....
....
....
....
....

Silent Endings

"Every new beginning comes from some other beginning's end." - Seneca

8. Reading: Matthew 4:12-17

Historians speculate that John the Baptist was imprisoned for about two years before his execution. During this time, John hears nothing from Jesus. There is no prison visit; Jesus remains silent. The silence is so deafening that John sends two of his disciples to inquire as to whether Jesus is the Messiah John preached about or if they should seek another (Matthew 11:1-6). The obvious conclusion is that John is feeling low, perhaps even depressed – after all, he is in prison. This seems plausible because Jesus is the Christ, so why hasn't He visited John, sent a word of encouragement for His cousin, or orchestrated a dramatic escape?

In reading 6, *Humility in the Wilderness*, we learned that John's purpose was to be the forerunner for Jesus. He fulfilled this role boldly and humbly. If we re-examine the timeline of events, we see that John baptises Jesus who is then led into the wilderness. As Jesus' ministry begins, John is arrested. His purpose has been fulfilled; it is Jesus' time to take centre stage. Is John doubting whether he should be celebrating the completion of his purpose?

John's doubt challenges us to consider how we manage the endings in our own lives. We all love beginnings; they're like beautifully wrapped gifts that fill us with anticipation about what lies beneath the paper. Endings can feel less appealing because they often involve loss. But both ends of the spectrum are essential. If Jesus isn't born (a beginning), we don't have hope, and, if He isn't crucified (an ending), we are eternally separated. Rather than doubt, we should ask God if our purpose in a relationship, job, or ministry has been fulfilled. Matthew doesn't answer our questions about John's state of mind before his execution. Maybe Jesus' response to John's question re-ignites his faith – we don't know. But we can ask God to give us the courage and wisdom to manage our endings well.

Reflections

Is God drawing a particular season or relationship to an end? How do you know? How do you feel?

What emotional and spiritual strategies can you put in place to manage this ending?

....
....
....
....
....
....
....
....
....
....
....
....

Immediate Response

"Procrastination is the thief of time."
- Edward Young

9. Reading: Matthew 4:18-22

What stands out to you in today's reading? Do you notice the word that is repeated? Matthew records that when Jesus calls Peter and Andrew, and then James and John, both sets of brothers respond "immediately." Their response is at odds with our culture of financial security. They do not make excuses – although, seriously, who will run their businesses? How will they provide for themselves and their families? These are not trivial questions. Yet, Matthew says they "immediately" follow Jesus. Most of us can exhale; God will probably not ask us to leave our jobs to enter the ministry full-time or become missionaries. However, the disciples' immediate obedience should cause us to reflect on our own contribution to the Kingdom. The Great Commission in Matthew 28:19 applies to all of us.

It is easy to become complacent and allow the weight of spreading the Gospel to fall on the pastor and church leadership team. We have busy lives – school, work, raising children, caring for elderly parents – but there is an urgent message in the story: Spreading the Gospel should be the principal priority of every Christian who believes Jesus is returning.

When the four disciples are called by Jesus, they are at work earning a living. There is a distinct message in that in and of itself because 2 Thessalonians 3:10 says, "…If anyone is not willing to work, let him not eat." However, supporting the work of the Kingdom should supersede our pursuit of financial freedom or building our careers. Though most of us won't be called to official ministry, we should seek to evangelise in our spheres of influence, and one way we can do this is by giving our time.

Prayer

God, I believe that You are returning. Sharing this message with others should be our deepest desire. Give me an opportunity this week to share my faith with someone. Amen.

Reflections

Make a list of ways you can support your local church. Review your list and create a timeline to follow through on each item.

When you think of your own values, where does spreading the Gospel fit into them? Are there areas in your life where career, financial security, or other commitments tend to overshadow your spiritual responsibilities?

....
....
....
....
....
....
....

The Comfort of the King

"Blessed are those who mourn, for they will be comforted." - Matthew 5:4

10. Reading: Matthew 5:1-12

The Sermon on the Mount, delivered by Jesus, is one of the most profound teachings in the Gospels. Found in both Matthew and Luke, in Matthew's account, this sermon marks the beginning of Jesus' public ministry. Imagine if Jesus were a newly elected leader; this would be His first address to a nation burdened by centuries of oppression and longing for hope. Yet, this sermon is so much more than a political speech. It is a divine manifesto, a declaration of blessing to a people who have suffered under Roman rule and have yearned for the Messiah's arrival.

The Beatitudes, as we know them, are more than moral guidelines for Christians – remember, Christianity had not yet formed as a religion at this time. They are promises of comfort and blessings for a broken people. When Jesus says, "Blessed are those who mourn," and "Blessed are those who are persecuted for righteousness' sake" (Matthew (5:4; 10), He speaks directly to the hearts of His audience – people who have endured loss, persecution, and despair. His words are a balm to their souls, offering not just comfort, but a deep assurance that they are seen and loved by the Messiah.

In a world where leaders often seem disconnected from the struggles of ordinary people, Jesus' words are a powerful reminder that our King is different. He does not rule from a distant throne; He walks alongside the broken-hearted, offering genuine comfort and hope. The Beatitudes are a testament to Jesus' compassion and His deep understanding of our pain.

Jesus' sacrifice on the Cross is the ultimate comfort, promising that no matter the suffering we endure in this life, He sees us, He is with us, and He will one day return to take us into His eternal presence, free from all oppression and suffering.

Reflections

How does knowing that Jesus sees and understands your pain affect your relationship with Him?

In what ways can you reflect Jesus' compassion and comfort to those around you who are suffering?

How do the Beatitudes challenge your understanding of what it means to be blessed?

Practical Task

This week, reach out to someone you know who is going through a difficult time. Offer them a listening ear, a word of encouragement, or a prayer. Reflect on how this act of compassion helps you connect with the heart of Jesus.

....
....
....

A Different Kind of Bright

"You are the light of the world. A town city that is set on a hill cannot be hidden." - Matthew 5:14

II. Reading: Matthew 5:13-16

Jesus used two everyday essentials – salt and light – to teach His followers the power of their witness for the kingdom of God. Although both are connected, we will focus on Jesus' teaching about light.

If we need light, we switch a flip. Jesus' listeners did not have that luxury. Their source of light was the oil lamp. Therefore, Jesus' teaching about not putting our light under a basket but rather on a lampstand (Matthew 5:14) held contextual relevance that we might miss today. Jesus' teaching is pithy and filled with wisdom. Our usual takeaway is that we should tell others about Jesus and not shy away from spreading the Gospel because the world needs our light. But here are three other truths we can extract:

- The first place we should share the Gospel is with those in our immediate sphere of influence: our family and friends. Jesus says the lampstand gives light to "all who are in the house" (Matthew 5:15).
- We have no light if we don't pay our electricity bill. In Jesus' day, they likewise would not have had light without oil. Spiritually, we cannot shine God's light on others if we are not connected to its source.
- Our "good works" (Matthew 5:16) – acts of justice, compassion, and kindness – are not performed so that we get the glory. Instead, our works lead others to Christ.

Today more than ever, let your light shine boldly, fuelled by your connection to God, so that through your words, actions, and love, others are drawn to glorify God and experience His transformative grace.

Reflections

How brightly does your light shine in your immediate circle of influence? Are there ways you can better reflect Christ's love to your family and friends?

Are you spiritually connected to the source of your light? What practices help you stay close to God, allowing His light to shine through you?

Do your actions and good works point others to Christ, or do they point to you? How can you ensure that your life glorifies God rather than seeking recognition for yourself?

....
....
....
....
....
....
....
....
....

True Righteousness

"Righteousness exalts a nation,
but sin is a reproach to any
people."
- Proverbs 14:34

12. Reading: Matthew 5:17-20

Jesus' listeners would have been familiar with the law handed down to Moses. The religious leaders of the time prided themselves on their meticulous adherence to this law. However, while they were experts in observing the law outwardly, they missed its deeper purpose. Jesus starts His teaching by affirming the law's ongoing relevance and permanence, making it clear that He has not come to abolish it but to fulfil it in its entirety.

In verse 19, Jesus gives a stern warning to anyone who breaks the commandments or leads others to do so. But the focus of today's reflection lies in verse 20, where Jesus shifts to the spirit behind the law – a concept the religious leaders failed to grasp.

The religious leaders of Jesus' time, the Pharisees and scribes, were known for their strict observance of the law. If there were awards for law-keeping, they undoubtedly would have won. Yet, they misunderstood that the law is not merely a set of rules to be followed but a divine tool meant to transform the heart. This is why, as we will see in the next reading, Jesus goes beyond the letter of the sixth commandment, "You shall not murder" (Exodus 20:13), to address anger that festers in the heart – a more subtle but equally dangerous form of breaking the law.

Jesus' teaching in Matthew 5:20 points us to a truth that the Pharisees missed: True righteousness is not about outward appearances or ritualistic adherence to the law. It's about an inward transformation that only the Holy Spirit can bring. The righteousness Jesus calls us to is one that surpasses mere performance. It is a righteousness that flows from a heart changed by God – a heart that reflects the love, mercy, and justice of the lawgiver Himself.

None of us can achieve this level of righteousness on our own. It is only through the work of the Holy Spirit in us that we can move beyond the superficial righteousness of the Pharisees and embrace the true righteousness that Jesus calls us to. This is not about ticking boxes but rather allowing God to change us from the inside out, so that our actions naturally align with His will.

Reflections

In what ways do you see yourself focusing on the outward observance of rules rather than allowing God's Word to transform your heart?

How can you invite the Holy Spirit to work in your life to help you move beyond superficial righteousness?

What does Jesus' teaching about true righteousness reveal about His understanding of our inner struggles and the power of grace?

....
....
....
....

Murder in the Heart

"To forgive is to set a prisoner free and discover that the prisoner was you." - Lewis B. Smedes

13. Reading: Matthew 5:21-26

*I*f you were to search the number of murders and attempted murders that have taken place since the start of the year, it would reveal that, for some, human life is not sacred. Sadly, the inviolable sacredness of human life was lost with the first murder (Genesis 4), and, since that moment, the value of life has only progressively diminished. Individuals have been murdered merely because they looked at someone for too long, because jealous lovers feel slighted and can't move on, or as revenge for actual or perceived wrongs.

During the Sermon on the Mount, Jesus went beyond the obvious claim that murder is wrong. Everyone in the crowd would have been familiar with the sixth commandment (Exodus 20:13). Jesus pushes them to see past the surface of that commandment and disrupts their traditional interpretation of it. Jesus says that murder is not just a physical act. He confronts the quiet anger inside us that has no righteous cause, the insults we speak, and the ill-feeling that is left to fester even as we appear saint-like on the outside. Jesus is dealing with the root of what would make someone *want* to commit murder. In the sermon's closing, Jesus says something interesting: If we are at the altar and remember that our brother has something against us, we should go and reconcile. We should not be the focus of attention if we're living righteously; it should be others. The Gospel is centred on others. These are not teachings for the selfish or prideful.

Maybe as you read this you feel that there is someone you have murdered in your heart. Don't ignore this feeling. Take time in today's reflection and in prayer to resolve it.

Reflections

How do you define the value of life in your everyday interactions? Are there ways in which your thoughts or words may undermine its value?

Take some time to allow God to reveal if there is someone you need to reconcile with.

How can you practice the Gospel's call to centre others in your acts and relationships?

....
....
....
....
....
....
....
....
....
....
....
....

Safeguarding Purity

"Purity is not about perfection, but about the direction of your heart-choosing to honor yourself, others, and the values that guide you in love and respect." - Unknown

14. Reading: Matthew 5:27-30

*I*n a 2001 article titled "Naked Capitalists," published in *The New York Times*, the American essayist Frank Rich explains why pornography is a pandemic that we must learn to live with. Unsurprisingly, Jesus disagreed. Immediately after He tackled the issue of anger, Jesus dealt with the sin of lust. Although Jesus addressed men, women are struggling, too. In fact, in her 2018 book, *Sex, Jesus and the Conversations the Church Forgot*, Mo Isom writes openly about her struggle with pornography and masturbation.

The heart of these two verses from Matthew is that we must fight for sexual purity and put safeguards in place to protect it. We cannot take a laissez-faire approach because lust untamed will get out of control.

Jesus again pushed His listeners to see beyond the commandment and set a higher standard. He says that if you lust after a woman, you have committed adultery in your heart. Then, Jesus paints a vivid and violent image to emphasise the point. Jesus says, "If your right eye causes you to sin, pluck it out..." (Matthew 5:29). Here, Jesus is addressing what we put before our eyes deliberately, but also inadvertently. Consider how many sexualised images we come across during a day. We are still – even if it is not our fault – responsible for controlling the lust this might evoke in us. The act of tearing out your eye is active, so there is an onus on us to be proactive.

How painful might some of us find having to revert to a 'dumb' phone that prevented access to the Internet? For many of us, this choice would feel violent. Yet, denying our temptations is better than eternal separation from Christ.

We live in a sinful world, and we have a fallen nature. Until Jesus returns, we will struggle with the temptation of sexual sin, but we do not have to succumb to it. To walk around without an eye or hand might raise questions. But could Jesus have been suggesting that we need to be open with those we trust about our areas of sexual weakness, as sin breeds most in the dark?

Reflections

What safeguards can you put in place to protect yourself from sexual sin?

How could viewing every human being as a child of God help with sexual sin?

....
....
....
....
....
....

Preparing for a Lifelong Love

"And a threefold cord is not quickly broken." - Ecclesiastes 4:12

15. Reading: Matthew 5:31-32

*I*n today's reading Jesus addresses the divine purpose of marriage. God intended marriage to be a lifelong covenant; it is a symbol of His relationship with us, the church. A literal interpretation of these three verses provides the following three guidelines for divorce:

1. Divorce can only occur if there is "sexual immorality" (Matthew 5:32).
2. A woman who is divorced for any other reason has committed adultery – even if it wasn't her choice.
3. Anyone who marries a woman who is divorced (except for reasons of adultery) also commits adultery.

Many churches now permit divorce if there has been abuse, and some churches will allow remarriage under these circumstances while others will not. If we are married, we hope these verses never apply to us. And those who are separated or divorced – even if the reason is not adultery – know the pain divorce causes. It is easy to get caught up in debates about when divorce can occur, but the better discussion is about how we can prepare couples to remain happily married.

Here are some suggestions, taken from the teachings of Jesus that we have explored so far:

- Couples need to be taught conflict resolution to ensure that they deal with hurt and unmet expectations so that anger does not fester and build.
- Each spouse is responsible for safeguarding their sexual purity in marriage. Honest conversations about past sexual experiences, any trauma, and expectations are necessary to encourage transparency.
- Successful marriages keep their salt. The moment couples stop doing what they did to attract each other, the marriage will lose its metaphorical taste and become tasteless. Couples should be encouraged to keep exploring, learning, and being curious about each other.

Finally, while God never intended divorce to occur, He understands each personal circumstance. If divorce has happened, God's love and care for those individuals does not diminish nor does His purpose and provision for their lives.

Reflections

How do I view the sacredness of marriage in my own life or in the lives of those around me?

What steps am I taking to safeguard my relationship, whether it be conflict resolution, maintaining intimacy, or upholding purity? Or, if you are unmarried and wish to marry, how are you preparing for marriage?

How can I use my experience as a divorced person to help others who might be considering divorce?

Our Word Should Be Enough

"A promise made is a debt unpaid."
- Robert W. Service

16. Reading: Matthew 5:33-37

*I*n Matthew 5:33-37, Jesus talks about the importance of having integrity in our words. He is not condemning all oaths but urging sincerity and truthfulness in speech, eliminating the need for oaths. A person with integrity is not just honest but also trustworthy and reliable. Here is what the author of *7 Habits of Highly Effective People*, Stephen Covey, says about integrity:

"While integrity means honesty, it's much more. It's integratedness. It's walking your talk. It's being congruent, inside and out."

In the passage, Jesus says that we should keep our promise to God; we should not swear on heaven or earth – because both belong to God. Instead, our yes and no should be sufficient. Let's apply this to our everyday relationships. As Christians, we should be known for keeping our promises, and people should be able to trust us. We should not need to make extravagant promises. Our word should be enough.

One reason a person might feel they have to swear on things – we hear people say, "I swear on my mother's life" – is because they have not previously walked in integrity and so feel that their word is not sufficient; they may have let others down in the past to the point people are slow to trust them now. The good news is that integrity can be rebuilt, and, although it will not be easy, we need not permanently dwell in our past lack of integrity. The Gospel of Christ is about restoration and transformation.

Finally, if we make a promise and later find we cannot fulfil it, we should be honest and see how we can make amends.

Reflections

How would those closest to you describe your trustworthiness?

Are there promises you have made to God and not kept? How can you remedy this?

....
....
....
....
....
....
....
....
....
....
....
....
....

The Extra Mile

"Go the extra mile. It's never crowded." - Wayne Dyer

17. Reading: Matthew 5:38-42

Given the limits of our human strength, the teachings in Matthew 5:38-42 are hard – if not impossible – to live out. Naturally, none of us want to allow someone who has hurt us before to do it again. Yet Jesus challenges His followers with a radical message, urging them to respond to evil in a way that goes beyond mere human logic or justice.

The concept of "an eye for an eye and a tooth for a tooth" (known as *lex talionis*) is rooted in the Old Testament (Exodus 21:24; Leviticus 24:20; Deuteronomy 19:21). It was designed to limit retribution and ensure that a punishment was proportional to the offense. While this law was meant to curb excessive reprisal, Jesus invites His followers to go even further by not just avoiding retaliation but embracing a spirit of grace and generosity.

Jesus' audience would have been familiar with the Roman law referenced in Matthew 5:41. Under this law, a Roman soldier could compel a Jewish man to carry his gear for one mile. Understandably, this law was a source of resentment among the Jews, as it symbolised their subjugation and oppression. But Jesus instructs His followers not just to comply with the law but to exceed it by going a second mile willingly. This extra mile is more than just physical distance; it's about a transformation of the heart that first changes the heart of the oppressed and then, hopefully, the heart of the oppressor.

This teaching, however, is not about passively accepting abuse. It's about breaking the cycle of revenge and hostility by responding with a love that disarms and transforms. Jesus is calling His followers to a higher standard, one that can only be achieved by relying on His strength and the power of the Holy Spirit within us.

Hebrews 4:15 reminds us, "…we do not have a high priest who is unable to sympathise with our weaknesses, but one who in every respect has been tempted as we are, yet without sin." Jesus is our perfect example, having endured suffering and temptation without yielding to sin. His life models how we too can respond to adversity with grace and strength when we rely fully on God.

It is not easy to love people when they hurt us, whether intentionally or unintentionally. But Jesus, our perfect example, has shown us that it is possible. And the good news is that we are not expected to do this in our own strength. He has equipped us with everything we need to love even the most challenging of people through Him.

Reflections

How does Jesus' example challenge your understanding of justice?

What situations in your life require you to go the extra mile for someone who has wronged you?

How can you rely more on Jesus' strength and the Holy Spirit to respond with grace in difficult situations?

Practical Task

This week, identify a situation where you feel wronged or mistreated. Instead of reacting in the way you typically would, choose to go the extra mile by responding with kindness or generosity. Reflect on how this affects your perspective and the situation itself.

Private Givers

"Real generosity is doing something nice for someone who will never find out." - Frank A. Clark

18. Reading: Matthew 6:1-4

Several years ago, *Forbes* published a list of the 30 most generous celebrities. The article noted that, "It's no surprise that celebrities like to have their name associated with good causes. It's good PR, and the more good they do, the more the public loves them."

Yet, in Matthew 6:1-4, Jesus gives a very different instruction to His followers: to give in secret. He even goes so far as to say that our giving should be so private that our right hand doesn't know what the left hand is doing.

There are important lessons in these verses. First, Jesus assumes that Christians will naturally be generous and give to those in need. Giving should be a part of our daily lives. But Jesus also anticipates that pride might creep in, leading us to give in ways that draw attention to ourselves. This is why He stresses the importance of giving privately.

Jesus' teaching challenges us to examine our motives for giving. Are we doing it to genuinely help those in need, or are we seeking recognition and praise from others?

Our hearts are prone to pride, and, to guard against this, God has set up checks to protect us and the dignity of those we help. No one likes to feel dependent on others, and by keeping our giving private, we respect the dignity of those we are supporting and ensure that we are giving for the right reasons.

Prayer

Dear God, help me to be a generous giver who helps others in need while keeping my heart humble. Remind me that I can only give because You have blessed me with the ability to earn. May my giving always bring honour to You and dignity to others. Amen.

Reflections

What were your true motives the last time you gave? Were they in line with Jesus' teachings?

How can you ensure that your giving is done in a way that honours God and respects the dignity of those you help?

Reflect on a time when you gave in secret. How did it feel compared to when your giving was known by others?

....
....
....
....
....
....
....

The Covenant of Prayer

"To be a Christian without prayer is no more possible than to be alive without breathing." - Martin Luther

19. Reading: Matthew 6:8-13

Prayer is often misunderstood in our culture. Sometimes it's seen as a mere wish list presented to God. However, prayer is far more profound than a list of wishes; it is the most powerful tool we have to connect with God and enact change on earth. Recognising its importance, Jesus taught His disciples not just the act of praying but also the feelings and intentions that should support it.

In the Bible, a covenant is a solemn agreement between God and humanity, involving promises, commitments, and obligations on both sides. Throughout Scripture, we see covenants such as the Noahic Covenant, Abrahamic Covenant, Mosaic Covenant, and ultimately, the New Covenant established by Christ.

In the passage we read today, Jesus is not merely giving His disciples a formulaic prayer but modelling one that reflects profound covenantal piety. The term 'piety' refers to a deep respect and reverence for God, coupled with a sincere desire to fulfil our covenantal obligations. When we examine the Lord's Prayer through this lens, it becomes clear that prayer is not primarily about asking God for things. Instead, it is a sacred connection with our Heavenly Father, intended to align our will with His and to bring His Kingdom to earth.

For instance, when Jesus teaches us to pray, "Your kingdom come, Your will be done on earth as it is in heaven," He is inviting us into God's covenantal mission to bring about divine justice, mercy, and love on earth. Every petition in the Lord's Prayer reflects this covenantal relationship – we seek our daily bread, not just for sustenance, but as a recognition of our dependence on God; we ask for forgiveness, not only to cleanse ourselves but to extend that grace to others as part of our covenant with Him.

Reflections

How does understanding prayer as part of a covenant with God change your approach to it?

In what ways does the Lord's Prayer help you to align your desires with God's will?

What does it mean to you to pray for God's Kingdom to be on earth as it is in heaven?

....
....
....
....
....
....
....
....

Where is Your Treasure?

"The more of heaven we cherish,
the less of earth we covet."
- David Jeremiah

20. Reading: Matthew 6:19-21

To discern what truly matters to someone, we need only observe what they talk about most, how they spend their time, and where they allocate their money. Matthew 6:21 is crucial for us as Christians because it speaks directly to the heart of our priorities. Jesus makes it clear: "For where your treasure is, there your heart will be also." It's important to understand the term 'heart' as it is used in this context. The original Greek word, *kardia*, refers to our thoughts and feelings. This insight gives us a deeper understanding of what Jesus is implying about our priorities.

Verses 19 and 20 provide context as to why it's essential to know where our treasure lies. In Matthew 6:19-20, Jesus instructs us not to store up treasures on earth but to lay them up in heaven. He provides both a focus and a reason: Earthly treasures are fleeting, but what we invest in heaven endures eternally. This teaching highlights the lasting value of our actions and offers guidance on how to manage our resources wisely.

This message transcends financial status. For a wealthy Jew listening at the time, Jesus was offering advice on how to use their wealth wisely. The Old Testament is rich with commands to care for the poor, but Jesus' message also resonates with those who have less and those striving to accumulate wealth by reminding them that their primary focus should not be on material gain.

God is not against wealth, but He doesn't want money – or anything – to capture our heart more than He does.

Reflections

If Jesus were to review your bank statements, what would they reveal about where your treasure lies?

Why does Jesus place such emphasis on how we spend our money? Is it truly ours?

The Antidote to Worry

"Worry does not empty tomorrow of its sorrow. It empties today of its strength." - Corrie Ten Boom

21. Reading: Matthew 6:25-34

A recent study by the World Health Organisation estimates that approximately 301 million people – around 4% of the global population – suffer from an anxiety disorder. Worry and anxiety not only take a toll on our mental health but can also weaken our immune system. Worry is a real problem. Even before the COVID-19 pandemic, there was plenty to worry about: family, money, relationships, work. Now, in the aftermath, financial insecurity due to the cost-of-living crisis is a pressing concern for most households.

Most Christians are familiar with Matthew 6:25-34, or the 'do not worry' passage from Jesus' Sermon on the Mount. We read it and, hopefully, feel reassured by Jesus' promise that our needs will be provided for. Jesus uses the example of the birds and the lilies of the field, which are cared for by God, to remind us how much more valuable we are to Him.

However, what can often be overlooked is the solution to worry that Jesus provides in Matthew 6:33: "But seek first the kingdom of God and His righteousness, and all these things will be added to you." If you've ever searched frantically for something like lost keys or a wallet, you know how consuming that search can be. That's the level of intensity God wants us to have in seeking His kingdom and righteousness. The term 'righteousness' refers to living rightly, with integrity and purity of character – these are the pursuits that should replace our worries. The promise is clear: As we learn to prioritise God's Kingdom and righteousness, He will take care of everything else we need.

Reflections

What is your usual approach to dealing with worry?

How can you practically apply Jesus' solution the next time you feel anxious?

Make a list of your worries, and, for each one, find a Bible verse where God promises to handle it for you.

....
....
....
....
....
....
....
....
....
....
....
....
....

Beyond Appearances

"What lies behind us and what lies before us are tiny matters compared to what lies within us."
- Ralph Waldo Emerson

22. Reading: Matthew 7:21-23

*I*n reading 10, *The Comfort of a King*, Jesus' opening in The Sermon on the Mount was compared to a political leader's first speech after getting into office. Jesus' words in this passage can seem harsh at first glance; however, with the right theological understanding, they are actually a compassionate warning about the true nature of faith and obedience. Throughout the Sermon on the Mount, Jesus redefines what it means to live as a part of God's Kingdom. Here, He brings His teaching to a conclusion by making it clear that mere outward actions, even those that seem spiritual, are not enough. What God desires is a heart that truly knows Him and seeks to do His will.

The phrase 'Kingdom of Heaven' is used in two key ways in the Gospels. First, it refers to the future hope of God's full reign when Jesus returns and the world is renewed. But it also describes a present reality – God's reign in the lives of those who follow Him. When Jesus speaks of those who will enter the Kingdom of Heaven, He is talking about those who live under God's rule here and now, allowing their hearts and lives to be transformed by His love and truth.

In Matthew 7:21-23, Jesus is challenging His listeners – and us today – to examine the true state of our hearts. Are we simply going through the motions of religious activity, or are we genuinely living in a way that reflects God's Kingdom? Are we doing the will of the

Father, or are we relying on our efforts to appear righteous? This passage reminds us that God is not impressed by outward displays of spirituality but is looking for hearts that are truly committed to Him.

Reflections

What does it mean to you to do 'the will of the Father' in your daily life?

How can you ensure that your relationship with God is genuine and not just based on outward actions?

How does understanding the Kingdom of Heaven as a present reality affect the way you live?

....
....
....
....
....
....
....
....
....
....
....
....

The Power of Submission

"There is no safer place to be than in the center of God's will."
- Charles Stanley

23. Reading: Matthew 8:1-13

The story of the leper in Matthew 8 reminds us that Jesus cares deeply for those whom society overlooks – the outcasts, the sick, and the marginalised. This is a profound encouragement for anyone who feels they are on the fringes of society's acceptance or care. God sees you, and He loves you. However, as we delve deeper into this narrative, we uncover something truly beautiful: the convergence of worship, humility, and the alignment of our will with God's.

Matthew writes, "And behold, a leper came and worshipped Him, saying, 'Lord, if You are willing, You can make me clean'" (Matthew 8:2). Notice first that the leper worships before making any request. This should prompt us to ask: How often do we approach God with adoration before presenting our needs? The leper's worship wasn't distinct from his request; his request was interwoven with faith and humility, and he wholly surrendered to God's will. How much faith do we bring when we come to God with our requests? And, perhaps more challengingly, how willing are we to submit to God's answer? Do we come with an entitled heart, or one that is open and submissive?

In this passage, we witness a beautiful convergence of wills – the leper's desire to be healed meets God's desire to heal. The leper says, "If You are willing," and Jesus responds, "I am willing; be cleansed" (Matthew 8:3). This moment of alignment between the leper's request and God's will is a powerful reminder that God's will is always at work, even within our prayers. Though God may not always say yes to our prayers, these are the moments when our faith is truly tested. Yet, if we can find a way to keep our hearts as joyful in unanswered prayers as in answered ones, we begin to demonstrate true submission to God's perfect will in our lives.

Reflections

When was the last time you worshipped God before making a request? How might this change your prayer life?

How would you feel if someone constantly asked you for things without ever acknowledging who you are? Does this reflect your approach to God?

What do you believe is more important in prayer – faith or submission? How can you cultivate a balance of both in your relationship with God?

....
....
....
....
....
....
....
....

The Battle We Cannot See

"Our battles are won by Him who
has already triumphed over all."
- Anonymous

24. Reading: Matthew 8:28-34

Spiritual warfare is real, and it happens in the unseen realm. We may not perceive it with our physical eyes – unless God allows us to – but it is undeniably occurring. Matthew's Gospel does not shy away from recounting Jesus' encounters with demonic forces. In Matthew 8:28-34, Jesus arrives in the country of the Gergesenes, where He meets two men described as "demon-possessed" (Matthew 8:28). We are told two significant details about these nameless men: They live among the tombs, and they are so violent that no one dares to pass by that way. These men are surrounded by death and utterly isolated, which should evoke in us great compassion for those who are oppressed by demonic forces or deceived into engaging with the occult and witchcraft.

A striking moment in this passage occurs when the demons recognise and address Jesus by His true title. They cry out, "What have we to do with You, Jesus, You Son of God?" (Matthew 8:29). This is further evidence that the spiritual realm exists and demonic forces recognise the power of Jesus. Interestingly, the demons plead with Jesus to send them into a herd of swine, indicating that they need a physical host to inhabit.

Perhaps the most disheartening part of this story is the reaction of the townspeople after the men are delivered. Instead of celebrating their freedom, they ask Jesus to leave. The narrative doesn't explain their reasons explicitly, but we can infer it was due to financial loss

– the swine were valuable. However, what is clear from this passage is that Jesus cares immensely about ensuring those that are held in spiritual prisons are freed and therefore so should we.

Reflections

How does the description of the demon-possessed men living among tombs reflect the spiritual isolation and torment experienced by those under demonic influence or spiritual oppression today?

The demons immediately recognised Jesus as the Son of God. How does this challenge us to reflect on our own recognition and acknowledgment of Jesus' authority in our lives?

What might the townspeople's reaction to Jesus reveal about our own priorities when we are confronted with the cost of spiritual freedom?

Practical Task

This week, spend time in prayer for those who are spiritually oppressed or involved in occult practices. Ask God to bring them into the light of His freedom, and pray for protection over your own spiritual life, committing to stand firm in the authority of Jesus Christ.

....
....
....

Making Room for the New

"God is always doing something new. We must learn to recognize and be willing to step into His newness." - Christine Caine

25. Reading: Matthew 9:16-17

Matthew 9 is a chapter full of transformation. We see the author, Matthew himself, accept Jesus, and witness the renewal of several lives: the paralytic man, Jairus' daughter, the woman with the issue of blood, the two blind men, and the mute man. The common thread in these stories is that each individual, after encountering Jesus, is made new. But this renewal doesn't come without a cost. They must relinquish their old ways, ideas, and beliefs, embracing the newness that Jesus offers.

Jesus illustrates this through the analogy of the wineskins. In those days, wine was stored in animal skins, which would stretch as the wine fermented. New wine, still fermenting and expanding, had to be put into new wineskins that could stretch along with it. If you put new wine into old wineskins, the old skins would burst because they couldn't handle the pressure, ruining both the wine and the skins. Jesus uses this metaphor to teach us that our old ways of thinking, living, and being cannot contain the new life He brings. To fully experience the transformation Jesus offers, we must be willing to let go of the old and embrace the new.

None of the individuals in Matthew 9 would have experienced transformation if they had clung to the old. The woman who could not stop her bleeding would not have been healed if she hadn't dared to reach out and touch Jesus' garment, believing in a new source of healing. Matthew would not have become an apostle – or written this very Gospel – if he had continued in his old life as a tax collector. Jairus had to put aside his status and admit that he needed Jesus to save his daughter. Each of these stories teaches us that God's renewal requires us to make room by letting go of the old.

What is it that God is asking you to release so that He can bring something new into your life? Are there old 'wineskins' in the form of outdated beliefs, habits, or ways of living that need to be discarded? Jesus offers us new life, but it requires us to be willing to stretch, grow, and transform.

Reflections

What 'old wineskins' in your life – whether they be habits, mindsets, or behaviours – might you need to discard to make room for God's new work in you?

How might clinging to old ways be hindering the new things God wants to do in your life?

Reflect on a time when you let go of something old to embrace something new. How did it change you?

....
....
....
....
....

Valued and Seen

"The true measure of any society can be found in how it treats its most vulnerable members." - Mahatma Gandhi

26. Reading: Matthew 9:18-26

In Jesus' time, women were often marginalised, considered less important in both social and religious contexts. Sadly, this marginalisation persists in various parts of the world today. However, in today's passage, Jesus puts women at the very centre, demonstrating that they are not only seen and valued but are recipients of His healing and love.

The narrative intertwines two powerful stories: the healing of Jairus' daughter and the woman whose bleeding could not be stopped. Through these stories, Jesus sends a profound message to all women: You are seen, loved, and cherished by God.

Here are some key lessons:

1. **A Father's Love:** Jairus, a synagogue leader, represents the ideal of a loving father who seeks the best for his daughter, even going to great lengths to secure her healing. This speaks to the importance of fathers in providing emotional and physical safety for their daughters. Yet, where this ideal falls short, God steps in as the ultimate Father. The nameless woman, whom society overlooked, is tenderly addressed by Jesus as "daughter," inviting all women to accept their place as cherished daughters of God (Matthew 9:22).

2. **Pursuit of Wellness:** The bleeding woman had suffered for 12 long years, exploring every possible avenue for healing. This demonstrates the importance of actively seeking wellness, whether through medical help, therapy, or other avenues. Yet, it also highlights that some healing can only come from God. Her faith and determination led her to Jesus, who alone could restore her fully.
3. **God's Timing in Healing:** The contrast between the woman's 12 years of suffering and Jairus' daughter's brief illness reminds us that God's healing is not bound by time. Whether immediate or delayed, God's intervention is perfect in its timing. We are called to trust His process, knowing that as a loving Father He will do what is best for us.

Jesus consistently affirmed the worth of women throughout His ministry. Even on the Cross, He ensured provision for His mother (John 19:25-27), and, after His resurrection, it was women who first received the news from the angel (Matthew 28:1-8). Women matter deeply to God, and He sees, values, and loves them.

Reflections

Which part of this story speaks most deeply to you, and why?

If you have a daughter, how can you ensure she feels valued and seen in her daily life?

In what ways do you pursue wellness, and how do you balance seeking help from others with relying on God for ultimate healing?

Practical Task

This week, take a moment to affirm the value of a woman in your life – whether it's your daughter, wife, sister, or a friend. Let her know that she is seen, loved, and valued by both you and God. If you're a woman, take time to reflect on your own worth in God's eyes and seek His healing and affirmation in areas where you may feel overlooked or undervalued.

How Will You Be Described?

"We each influence around 80,000 people throughout our lives, enough to fill a stadium. How will those 80,000 people remember us at the end of our days? Our legacy is our choice."
- Tommy Spaulding

27. Reading: Matthew 10:1-4

How would those closest to you describe you? In Matthew 10:4, we are introduced to Judas Iscariot with the foreboding description, "…and Judas Iscariot, who also betrayed Him." It's a sobering introduction – one that marks Judas forever as the betrayer. It's uncomfortable and should inspire us to consider how we might be remembered and, more importantly, how Jesus will speak of us before the Father at the end of time.

Judas had a remarkable opportunity. He was chosen by Jesus and given the privilege of being close to Him, witnessing His miracles, hearing His teachings, and participating in His ministry. Despite this incredible proximity to the Son of God, Judas' heart remained unchanged. He clung to self-interest and his love for money, a stark contrast to Matthew, the former tax collector. Matthew, who once defrauded others for personal gain, encountered Jesus and found that the pursuit of wealth and comfort was ultimately empty. He chose to follow Christ leaving his old ways behind.

There are three powerful lessons we can learn from Judas' tragic story:

1. **God Offers Us Every Opportunity to Know Him:** Judas was not a mistake. He was chosen deliberately and given every chance to experience Jesus intimately. This shows that God will arrange circumstances in our lives

where we can encounter Him. The question is, how will we respond?
2. **God Respects Our Choices:** God is love, and true love respects free will. Judas had the choice to embrace Jesus fully or to follow his own desires. Even in the Garden of Eden, God gave Adam and Eve the freedom to choose, knowing that true love cannot be coerced. Our choices reveal the depth of our love for God.
3. **Anything We Love More than God Will Destroy Us:** Judas' love for money ultimately cost him everything. God will not override our choices, but while He accepts them, the consequences are real. Our priorities matter, and anything we place above God has the potential to lead us away from Him.

Reflections

It is easy to condemn Judas, but what in your life have you chosen, or are you currently choosing, over God?

How does the story of Judas challenge you personally in your walk with Christ?

....
....
....
....
....
....

The Cost of Discipleship: What Do You Love Most?

"When Christ calls a man, he bids him come and die. There is no cheap grace. The price of following Jesus is everything, and yet, some will sell Him for a moment's gain."
- Dietrich Bonhoeffer

28. Reading: Matthew 10:34-39

The teachings of Jesus in Matthew 10:34-39 challenge us to examine the depth of our commitment to Him. However, because Jesus is so loving, three times in Matthew 10:22-31, right before setting out what would be frightening for most of us, Jesus comforts and says, "Do not be afraid." Jesus' words may seem unsettling, especially when He declares that He has come not to bring peace, but a sword, setting family members against one another. This is not about inciting conflict for its own sake but about prioritising our love for Him above all else – even above those we hold dearest.

In Matthew 10:37, Jesus makes it clear that there can be no relationship that we value more than our one with Him. He specifically mentions our closest family members: father, mother, son, and daughter. These are the relationships where we should first experience love, security, and belonging. But Jesus' command extends beyond just these relationships. We could also add spouses, grandparents, friends, careers, or any other person or thing that we might be tempted to place above God. The call is simple yet profound: Nothing and no one should come before Him.

This teaching is consistent with the first commandment, which tells us to have no other gods (Exodus 20:3). These gods can take many forms: family, career, possessions, or status. If we cling too tightly to these, we risk making them idols, placing them in a position that only God should occupy. Jesus' warning is stark: If we love these more than Him, we are "not worthy of Him."

The repetition of the phrase "not worthy of Me" three times in this passage highlights the gravity of Jesus' message. He concludes with the challenge to take up our own cross and follow Him. The Cross is a symbol of sacrifice and total commitment and represents the cost of true discipleship. As we continue in our journey through the Book of Matthew, this theme will become even more evident, especially in reading 41, *Will You Follow?*, where we explore the implications of taking up our own cross in greater depth.

Christianity is not a soft or easy path. It demands our all – our allegiance, our love, our very lives. The question we must answer is whether we are willing to pay the price and be found worthy of Him.

Reflections

How do you feel knowing that Jesus may call you to place Him above those you love most?

Do you find Jesus' demand unfair, or do you see it as a necessary part of true discipleship?

What in your life currently competes with your love for God?

Practical Task

Spend time in prayer and reflection, asking God to reveal any areas of your life where you may be placing something or someone above Him. If He shows you anything, ask for the grace to reorder your loves and to place Him at the centre of your life.

A Lighter Load

"Cast your burden on the Lord, and he will sustain you; he will never permit the righteous to be moved."
- Charles Spurgeon

29. Reading: Matthew 11:28-30

*I*n Matthew 11:28-30, Jesus offers us an invitation that stands in contrast to the heavy burdens imposed by religious legalism. When Jesus says, "Come to Me, all you who labour and are heavy laden, and I will give you rest," He is addressing those who are weary from trying to earn their righteousness through rigid observance of the law and human traditions. The religious leaders of the time had burdened the people with countless rules, turning the Sabbath – a day intended for rest – into a source of anxiety and guilt.

The word 'burden' (*phortizō*) in the original Greek refers to the heavy load placed on a vessel or an animal. This burden symbolises the crushing weight of trying to achieve spiritual perfection through human effort. Jesus offers an alternative to this wearisome struggle: "Take My yoke upon you and learn from Me, for I am gentle and lowly in heart, and you will find rest for your souls. For My yoke is easy and My burden is light."

A yoke is a wooden frame that joins two animals, typically oxen, together to pull a plough or cart. By offering His yoke, Jesus invites us to be yoked with Him, to walk in step with Him, and to share in the work He has already accomplished. Unlike the yoke of legalism, which leads to exhaustion, Jesus' yoke brings relief and rest. His yoke is "easy" because it is not about religious performance but about a relationship with Him. His burden is "light" because He carries it with us, offering us grace instead of demands.

However, to experience this rest, we must do two things. Firstly, we must choose to take His yoke, which means consciously turning away from the old, burdensome system of trying to earn our way to God. Secondly, we must be willing to learn from Him, embracing His teachings and His example. Jesus assures us that as we do this, we will find rest for our souls. He describes Himself as "gentle and lowly in heart," the very opposite of the harsh and prideful religious leaders. Jesus' gentle and humble heart is the key to the rest He offers; it is an invitation to come as we are and find peace in His presence.

While Jesus promises rest, it is not a passive experience. We are invited into an active, living relationship with Him, where we learn to trust in His grace rather than our efforts.

Reflections

Make a list of religious practices or traditions you follow. Are they rooted in Scripture, or are they burdensome rituals you've taken on out of habit or obligation?

How does understanding Jesus' death on the Cross help you to embrace the rest He offers? How does it change your approach to faith?

Practical Task

Spend time in prayer asking Jesus to help you identify any areas in your spiritual life where you may be carrying unnecessary burdens. Ask Him to teach you how to rest in His grace and to lead you away from legalistic practices that do not bring true spiritual growth. Take one step today to release a burden you've been carrying and entrust it to Him.

Rule Keepers with Rigid Hearts

"The letter killeth, but the spirit giveth life." - Apostle Paul

30. Reading: Matthew 12:1-14

At first glance, the Pharisees' anger towards Jesus in Matthew 12 might seem justified – they were, after all, trying to uphold the Sabbath laws. However, a deeper look at the text reveals a far more troubling issue: Their anger was not rooted in a desire to honour God, but in jealousy, control, and a refusal to acknowledge that they had distorted the Sabbath into a burdensome ritual rather than a day of rest and blessing.

In this passage, we see Jesus and His disciples walking through grainfields on the Sabbath. When the disciples begin to pluck and eat the grain, the Pharisees accuse them of breaking the Sabbath law. But Jesus responds with examples from Scripture that show how even within the law, mercy and human need have always taken precedence. He reminds them of how David, when hungry, ate the consecrated bread meant only for priests, and how the temple priests themselves work on the Sabbath without guilt. Jesus then makes a profound declaration: "For the Son of Man is Lord even of the Sabbath" (Matthew 12:8).

This statement is a direct challenge to the Pharisees' authority. By declaring Himself Lord of the Sabbath, Jesus is asserting that God – not man – determines the true meaning and observance of the Sabbath. The Pharisees had become so fixated on rules and rituals that they completely missed the heart of God's law, which is centred on love, mercy, and compassion. Their reaction to Jesus' healing of the man with the withered hand in the synagogue further exposes their hearts. Instead of rejoicing at the miracle and the relief of suffering, they begin to plot how to destroy Him. This response reveals that their rigid rule-keeping had led them to a place where they were more concerned with their own power and control than with the well-being of others.

We must ask ourselves if there are ways in which we, too, prioritise rules and traditions over loving and serving others. Jesus shows us that love and mercy must always be at the forefront of our faith, even if it means challenging long-held practices or stepping outside our comfort zones.

Reflections

How can you ensure that your observance of religious practices reflects God's heart of mercy and not mere ritual?

Consider how Jesus' challenge to the Pharisees might apply to your life today. Are there areas where you need to re-evaluate your priorities?

....

....

....

....

....

....

....

Understanding Blasphemy

"Blasphemy is the most consummate of all sins because it is a violation of the very spirit of faith." - Thomas Manton

31. Reading: Matthew 12:31-32

To fully understand this reading, we need to understand the context. The Pharisees, increasingly hostile towards Jesus, have just witnessed Him heal a man who was blind, mute, and demon-possessed. Instead of recognising this miracle as an act of God, they accuse Jesus of casting out demons by the power of Beelzebub, the prince of demons (Matthew 12:22-30). Jesus, knowing their thoughts, points out the absurdity of their accusation: A kingdom divided against itself cannot stand. The Pharisees' accusation wasn't just an error in judgment; it was a wilful and deliberate rejection of the Holy Spirit's work through Jesus.

Blasphemy, by definition, is speaking or acting in a way that shows disrespect or irreverence towards God. The Pharisees' charge against Jesus was not merely a mistake but a conscious choice to deny the obvious work of the Holy Spirit. Jesus' warning here is not about an isolated sin but a persistent, hardened attitude of unbelief – a refusal to acknowledge the Holy Spirit's power and presence.

New believers often worry that they might accidentally commit the unforgivable sin. However, what Jesus refers to here is not a one-time mistake but a deliberate and continuous rejection of the Spirit's work. The most heinous sins that we can imagine can be forgiven because of Christ's sacrifice on the Cross – even when others refuse to forgive or let us forget. What cannot be forgiven is the conscious decision to reject the Holy Spirit, the very source of grace and forgiveness.

The key to avoiding this sin lies in daily surrender to God. The Pharisees' refusal to believe stemmed from pride, the root of all sin. By humbling ourselves and recognising our need for God's grace, we remain open to the Spirit's work in our lives.

Reflections

How does pride affect your relationship with God and others?

Are there areas in your life where you might be resisting the Holy Spirit's guidance?

How can you cultivate a heart that is open and responsive to the Holy Spirit?

....
....
....
....
....
....
....
....
....

The Ongoing Journey of the Heart

"The longest journey is the journey inward." - Dag Hammarskjöld

32. Reading: Matthew 13:1-23

The Parable of the Sower is often viewed as a metaphor for how people respond to the Gospel when they first hear it. But what if we consider this parable an ongoing reflection of our spiritual journey, rather than just a one-time reaction to God's Word?

In Matthew 13, Jesus describes a sower scattering seeds, which represent the Word of God. These seeds fall on four types of ground: the wayside, stony places, thorny ground, and good soil. Each type of soil symbolises a different response to God's Word.

1. **The Wayside (Path):** This represents those who hear God's Word but do not understand it. Before it can take root, Satan snatches it away. The message never penetrates the heart, and the opportunity for spiritual growth is lost.
2. **Stony Places:** These hearers receive the Gospel with initial joy, but their faith has no deep roots. When persecution or hardship arises, their faith withers because it was only a superficial, emotional response.
3. **Thorny Ground:** This illustrates those who hear God's Word and believe but are overwhelmed by life's worries, materialism, and the pursuit of wealth. These distractions choke the Word, making the hearers unfruitful as they attempt to serve two masters.

4. **Good Soil**: This represents those who hear the Word, understand it, and are receptive to the Holy Spirit. They actively nurture and cultivate their relationship with God and bear much fruit, producing a harvest in their lives.

While this parable is typically interpreted through the lens of initial conversion, it can also serve as a daily litmus test for our relationship with God. Our walk with Christ isn't solely about the moment we first accept the Gospel; it's about our continuous response to God's voice in our lives. Every time we read Scripture, listen to a sermon, or engage with spiritual teachings, we have a choice: to embrace the message and let it take root, or to allow distractions, doubts, or worldly concerns to choke it out.

This parable challenges us to examine the condition of our hearts regularly. Jesus' parable reminds us that being good soil isn't a static state. It's a daily choice to cultivate a heart that is open, receptive, and eager to grow in God's truth. We must actively work to remove the 'thorns' and 'rocks' – those things that hinder our spiritual growth – so that God's Word can flourish within us.

Reflections

Which type of soil best represents the current state of your heart and why?

What 'thorns' or 'rocks' in your life are preventing God's Word from taking root and growing?

How can you cultivate a heart that is more receptive to God's Word on a daily basis?

When Familiarity Breeds Contempt

"No man is a hero to his own valet."
- Michel de Montaigne

33. Reading: Matthew 13:53-58

Have you ever had someone you went to school with or knew by association become famous? Did you think back to the less polished version of them? Maybe you remembered their flaws and awkward moments, and so struggled to reconcile who they were with who they'd become.

In Matthew 13, Jesus offers what our culture would call gems of wisdom – nuggets of truth we would do well to apply in our lives. Jesus returns to His hometown with the same message He has been preaching and that has transformed lives. We might expect Him to be welcomed as a hero, but His hometown reacts differently. Initially, they are amazed by His wisdom and mighty works, but that amazement quickly turns into offence when they remember His humble beginnings: "Isn't this the carpenter's son? Isn't His mother called Mary, and aren't His brothers James, Joseph, Simon, and Judas? And aren't all His sisters here with us?" (Matthew 13:55-56). Their familiarity with Jesus' background blinds them to His divinity and authority, leading them to reject Him.

Think back to reading 26, *Valued and Seen*, and the two miracles (the healing of the woman with the issue of blood and of Jairus' daughter) that took place. Yet, in His own hometown, Jesus does not get to perform any life-changing miracles. The people cannot receive healing because they are stuck on Jesus' humble beginnings, which creates unbelief and offence. What's behind their attitude?

Pride. Sadly, had the same message been delivered by someone they did not know, they would have readily accepted it, but instead they missed out on spiritual and physical transformation.

This is a powerful warning to us. God may choose to send guidance or blessings through the most unexpected channels. We must remain open-minded and receptive to whoever God chooses to use.

Reflections

What surprises you most about this story and why?

Have you ever responded like the people in Jesus' hometown to a person? What was behind your judgement?

....
....
....
....
....
....
....
....
....
....
....

More than a Beheading

"The blood of the martyrs is the seed of the church." - Tertullian

34. Reading: Matthew 14:1-12

When you read about the beheading of John the Baptist, it's easy to see it as nothing more than a brutal end to a faithful prophet's life. But there is so much more to this story. It is a powerful narrative about handling trials, rash decisions, the dangers of evil influence, and the reality of suffering for the Gospel.

1. **Handling Trials:** Scholars estimate that John was in prison for about two years. Put yourself in John's shoes; each day, he probably prayed – hoped – that somebody, maybe his cousin Jesus, would free him. Imagine how John felt when he realised there would be no rescue. What would you be thinking and feeling? Would your faith wane?

2. **The Cost of Rash Promises:** Herod made a rash promise when the dancing of Herodias' daughter enticed him. This teaches us that promises made when we are not in complete control of our senses can have devastating consequences.

3. **The Devil's Schemes:** The influence of evil is evident in Herodias' manipulation of her daughter to achieve her vengeful goal. This reminds us that the devil is always looking for opportunities to lead us into sin and destruction. We must be vigilant and discerning,

recognising when we are being lured into actions that go against God's will.

4. **The Influence of Parents:** Herodias' daughter, traditionally known as Salome, was drawn into a murderous scheme due to her mother's influence. This highlights the responsibility parents have in shaping the moral compass of their children. Herodias' vengeful and immoral behaviour left a lasting impact on her daughter, leading her to make a request that ended an innocent man's life. As parents, mentors, and leaders, we must be mindful of the example we set for those who look up to us.

The beheading of John the Baptist is challenging – it's not the end we want. But it teaches us that faithfulness to God does not exempt us from persecution, imprisonment, or even death. Our faith must be rooted in the power of the Cross, which is our transcending hope, even in the face of our most severe trials – including death.

Reflections

What stands out to you most in this story, and why?

Have you ever faced a situation where you expected God to intervene but found yourself continuing to wait? How did that impact your faith?

....

....

Sent into the Storm

"Faith means obedience regardless of the consequences." - Elisabeth Elliot

35. Reading: Matthew 14:22-33

Some of us have been exposed to teaching that says once we accept Jesus, we will be free from hardship and God will become our personal genie in a bottle. And yet, in Matthew 14:22-33, we read that Jesus intentionally sent the disciples into a storm. He then retreated to a mountain to pray, knowing the danger they faced. Our first question might be: Why would Jesus do that? But what if the better question is, what did the disciples learn during the storm?

The storm reveals the disciples' initial response to a crisis: fear, not prayer. Remembering that the storm came right after they witnessed Jesus feeding the 5,000 is crucial. It shows how forgetful we can be of God's goodness towards us and His provisions. They witness Jesus perform miracles, yet their first reaction in a crisis is to panic.

Jesus comes to the disciples in the storm even though they do not cry out specifically to Him. The text says they "…cried out in fear" (Matthew 14:26). God loves us and, even when we are paralysed with fear and do not know what to pray, He is near and is working things out for our good.

When Jesus appears, the disciples are not filled with faith, but with doubt. Even Peter, who asks to walk on water, does so as a test, still uncertain if it is truly Jesus. It's only when Peter begins to sink in fear that he cries out, "Lord, save me!" (Matthew 14:30), and Jesus rescues him. But don't miss this: The storm doesn't immediately cease when Jesus arrives. Could it be that Jesus was teaching them – and us – that His presence is enough, even when the storm rages on? Perhaps the greatest lesson in the storm is not the calming of the wind, but the calming of our spirits, knowing that God is with us.

Storms in life are not punishments, but opportunities to deepen our faith and trust in a sovereign God who is always at work, even as the storm rages on.

Reflections

How do you typically react when faced with a crisis? Is your first response fear or prayer?

Can you recall a time when you felt God's presence amid a storm? How did that experience shape your faith?

What might God be trying to teach you in your current circumstances, even if the storm hasn't yet calmed?

....

....

....

....

....

....

The Heart of the Matter

"What comes out of the mouth proceeds from the heart, and this defiles a person." - John Bunyan

36. Reading: Matthew 15:1-20

*I*n this passage, the Pharisees and scribes find yet another reason to criticise Jesus. This time, they question why His disciples do not follow the tradition of handwashing before eating. Jesus does not hold back in His response. In Matthew 15:18, He states, "But those things which proceed out of the mouth come from the heart, and they defile a man." Jesus' point is clear: The true issue isn't dirty hands but dirty hearts. The Pharisees were so obsessed with outward rituals that they failed to recognise the real problem – the condition of their hearts.

The Pharisees were known for their outward show of righteousness, but Jesus saw through to their hypocrisy. They were more concerned with keeping up appearances than with genuinely changing their hearts. Jesus is making it clear that He would rather have someone with unwashed hands and a pure heart than someone who is outwardly clean but inwardly corrupt.

This message is still relevant today. In a world where social media often pressures us to present a flawless image, it's easy to focus on the external while neglecting the internal. We can curate perfect snapshots of our lives, all while struggling with hidden sins and insecurities. But God isn't fooled by appearances. He's not interested in our polished exteriors; He's after our hearts. True transformation begins when we allow God to work on us inwardly, knowing that when our hearts are right, everything else will follow.

Reflections

In what ways might you be like the Pharisees, focusing on outward appearances rather than inner transformation?

What daily practices do you have in place to ensure that God has regular access to your heart?

Practical Task

Meditate on Psalm 139:23-24 to help you in your journey of introspection and heart transformation.

Spend five minutes each day this week in quiet reflection, asking God to reveal any areas in your heart that need His transforming power. Write down any insights and pray for strength to make the necessary changes.

....
....
....
....
....
....
....
....
....
....

Persistent Faith and Humility

"Faith is the bird that feels the light when the dawn is still dark."
- Rabindranath Tagore

37. Reading: Matthew 15:21-28

Matthew's account of the Gentile woman is more than just a story of a desperate mother seeking to have her daughter delivered from demonic possession. It's a powerful lesson in persistent faith, humility, and the rewards that such faith can bring.

This mother, a Gentile, approaches Jesus with a bold request to heal her daughter. The fact that she is a Gentile is crucial, especially since Matthew's Gospel is primarily written for a Jewish audience. Despite her background, she acknowledges Jesus as "Lord" and "Son of David," titles that even the Pharisees, who were well-versed in the scriptures, refused to recognise. However, Jesus initially responds by ignoring her, which seems out of character and even harsh. But the woman doesn't take offence; instead, she persists and goes even further by worshipping Him. How do we react when our prayers seem unanswered? Do we doubt, or do we press in with worship and trust?

When Jesus finally does respond, He reminds the woman of her position as a Gentile, implying that His mission primarily concerns the Jews. His words could have easily been taken as an insult, comparing her to a dog, but the woman's response is remarkable. She accepts her position and uses Jesus' own words to argue her case, showing humility and an unwavering belief in His power and goodness. Her response so impresses Jesus that He declares, "O woman, great is your faith!" and grants her request, healing her daughter instantly.

This passage challenges us to consider the depth of our own faith. Are we willing to be persistent in prayer, even when God seems silent? Are we humble enough to accept God's timing and His will, even when it means waiting longer than we'd like or hearing things that challenge us? The Gentile woman's faith is a model for us all, showing that humility, persistence, and faith can lead to blessings beyond our expectations.

Reflections

How does this passage encourage us to be persistent in prayer, even when we don't get immediate answers?

What other lessons might Jesus have been teaching through this interaction with the Gentile woman?

How should we handle situations where God's response isn't what we expected or wanted?

....
....
....
....
....
....
....

Remembering God's Faithfulness

"God's faithfulness means that God will always do what He has said and fulfill what He has promised."
- Wayne Grudem

38. Reading: Matthew 15:32-39

Jesus had been teaching a vast crowd of around 4,000 men, not counting women and children, for three days. The people were now hungry, but there was no food. Jesus, moved with compassion, said, "I feel sorry for these people… I don't want to send them away hungry, or they will faint along the way" (Matthew 15:32, NLT). The disciples' response would seem to be the logical one, where would we get enough food here in the wilderness for such a huge crowd? However, considering that Jesus had recently fed 5,000 people, their response would also seem to be lacking in faith. Surely, they should have thought, "Let's see if someone has any fish and loaves."

Even when they tell Jesus they have seven loaves and a few small fish, they still don't fully grasp that Jesus can feed this crowd. Jesus instructs the people to sit down; He gives thanks for the loaves and fish, breaks them into pieces, and then asks the disciples to distribute them.

This miracle should leave us in awe of God's compassion and provision. It also serves as a reminder that, like the disciples, we can be quick to forget God's past faithfulness. If the disciples had reflected on what Jesus had already done, they would have been bolder in their faith and possibly initiated this miracle themselves.

Reflections

Take a moment to jot down instances from the past three weeks where God has shown His faithfulness in your life. Are you similar to the disciples in forgetting what God has done for you in the past?

Practical Task

Spend time this week intentionally recalling and recording moments where God has provided for you or shown His faithfulness. Keep this list somewhere visible to remind yourself of His ongoing presence and care in your life.

....
....
....
....
....
....
....
....
....
....
....
....

Testing the Teachings

"Reader, as long as you live- resolve that you will read for yourself; think for yourself, judge of the Bible for yourself; in the great matters of your soul." - J.C. Ryle

39. Reading: Matthew 16:5-12

If you've ever baked bread, you know that yeast is a crucial ingredient. Yeast acts as a leavening agent, enabling the dough to rise and giving the bread its structure. Without yeast, the bread remains flat and dense. Referring to this process, Jesus warns His disciples, "Beware of the yeast of the Pharisees and Sadducees" (Matthew 16:6, NLT). Initially, the disciples misunderstand, thinking Jesus is speaking about literal bread. But soon, they grasp the deeper meaning: Jesus is cautioning them against the subtle and pervasive influence of the Pharisees' and Sadducees' teachings, which can easily corrupt the purity of the Word.

To understand why these teachings were so offensive to Jesus, we can look back to the Sermon on the Mount. To summarise: Firstly, it only takes a few false teachings to infiltrate and spoil true doctrine. Just as a little yeast makes the whole loaf rise, a minor distortion can have significant consequences. Secondly, false teaching leads people away from God, who should be our ultimate strength and source of truth. We only have to recall how Eve's slight alteration of God's command in the Garden of Eden led to disastrous consequences, demonstrating how even a small deviation from God's Word can lead to significant downfall.

It's crucial that we know God's Word intimately and refrain from blindly accepting the interpretations of those we regard as authorities – whether they are pastors, authors, or popular influencers. We each have the Holy Spirit as our guide, instructor, and teacher, and this should be our primary source of truth, rather than human intermediaries.

Reflections

How diligent are you in verifying what you hear in a sermon, read in a book, or encounter online?

What steps can you take to safeguard your understanding of God's Word in the future?

....
....
....
....
....
....
....
....
....
....
....
....
....
....
....

On Guard

"If you will tell me when God permits a Christian to lay aside his armour, I will tell you when Satan has left off temptation." - Charles Spurgeon

40. Reading: Matthew 16:21-23

As Christians, it's imperative that we recognise how Satan can influence any one of us at any time. Not every thought or idea that enters our minds is from God. That's why it is crucial to filter everything through the lens of God's Word – our best defence against negative influences.

In Matthew 16:22, Jesus begins to reveal the suffering He must endure to His disciples. In response, Peter, out of love and concern, exclaims, "Far be it from You, Lord; this shall not happen to You!" (Matthew 16:22). However, Jesus' response is striking. He doesn't rebuke Peter directly but rather addresses Satan, saying, "Get behind Me, Satan!" This moment is significant because it reveals that even those who love Christ deeply can have thoughts that are influenced by Satan.

Despite his love for Jesus, Peter found himself speaking words that were not aligned with God's will. This teaches us that no matter how long we've been walking with God, we can still misspeak or act in ways that don't align with Scripture. Therefore, it is essential that we consistently measure our words and actions against the Bible.

Our battle against Satan is not a one-time event but a daily struggle. We must be vigilant in guarding our hearts and minds, ensuring that we are not giving Satan any easy access through what we watch, listen to, and read. In a world filled with distractions and consumerism, safeguarding the avenues to our hearts is more crucial than ever.

Reflections

How can you be more discerning in filtering your thoughts and ideas through God's Word?

In what ways do you think Satan tries to influence your thoughts, and how can you guard against this?

Are there specific areas in your life where you need to be more vigilant about aligning your thoughts and actions with God's will?

Practical Task

Take time today to assess what you consume – whether it's media, books or our conversations. Ask yourself if these are in line with God's Word. Commit to making changes where necessary to ensure your heart and mind are more guarded against negative influences.

....
....
....
....
....
....

Will You Follow?

"Discipleship is the process of becoming who Jesus would be if he were you."
- Dallas Willard

41. Reading: Matthew 16:24-28

When you pick up a food product in the grocery store, the ingredients list on the back tells you what you're about to consume. Depending on your dietary needs, you might decide to either purchase the item or put it back on the shelf. In Matthew 16:24, Jesus offers us a different kind of ingredients list, one that outlines what it takes to be His disciple. To follow Him, He says, requires self-denial, suffering, and unwavering trust.

First, Jesus instructs, "…let him deny himself…" (Matthew 16:24). This is not a suggestion, but a requirement. We cannot follow Christ faithfully while clinging to our own desires, agendas, and plans. Our vision boards might need to be completely reimagined. The life of a disciple is about aligning ourselves with God's will, rather than trying to fit God into our plans. The act of self-denial is a daily decision to prioritise God's desires over our own.

Next, Jesus calls us to "take up his cross." The term 'his' is singular, indicating that each of us has our own cross to bear. In Roman times, the cross was a symbol of one of the most brutal forms of execution, representing suffering, shame, and death. For us, taking up our cross means a spiritual dying to self, and for some, it may even mean literal suffering or martyrdom. This part of the journey is not easy, but it is a necessary step in truly following Jesus.

Finally, Jesus says, "...and follow Me." He doesn't specify where this path will lead or what challenges we might face along the way. Following Jesus is an act of faith and requires trusting in Him even when the future is uncertain. If God were to show us everything we might endure, many of us might hesitate to commit. But Jesus calls us to trust Him without knowing all the details.

Each of these steps – self-denial, taking up our cross, and following Jesus – is an active, conscious choice. There is no room for passivity in true discipleship. Jesus has already paid the ultimate price for our sins, and, by asking us to take up our cross, He invites us into the rewards of His sacrifice – an intimate relationship with Him, a transformed character, and ultimately, eternal life.

Reflections

What personal desires or plans might you need to surrender to truly follow Jesus?

How do you respond to the idea of suffering as a part of discipleship? Are you willing to embrace it for the sake of Christ?

In what ways can you actively trust Jesus more, especially when the future is unclear?

Practical Task

Reflect on an area of your life where you've been holding onto control. Spend time in prayer, asking God to help you surrender this to Him and trust in His plan for you. Write down your commitment and revisit it regularly as you continue your journey of discipleship.

Warfare in the Spiritual Realm

"We are not human beings having
a spiritual experience; we are
spiritual beings having a human
experience."
- Pierre Teilhard de Chardin

42. Reading: Matthew 17:14-21

Throughout His ministry, Jesus consistently demonstrated His authority over demonic spirits, confidently delivering those who were oppressed by them. One such account is the story of the boy with epilepsy. From it, we can glean invaluable insights into the dynamics of spiritual warfare. The boy's father, desperate for his son's healing, brought him to Jesus after the disciples were unable to cast out the demon. When they later asked Jesus why they couldn't drive the spirit out, He pointed to their lack of faith. This highlights the importance of having faith when confronting demonic forces. Jesus further illustrates this by comparing faith to a mustard seed, teaching us that even the smallest measure of true faith holds tremendous power.

Jesus concludes the discussion with an interesting statement: "However, this kind does not go out except by prayer and fasting" (Matthew 17:21). The word 'however' here serves as a bridge, linking Jesus' earlier teachings on the power of faith to the necessity of prayer and fasting. This indicates that certain types of demonic spirits require not only faith but also the additional spiritual discipline of prayer and fasting to be effectively dealt with. It's a reminder that some spiritual battles are more intense and require deeper spiritual preparation.

Demonic warfare is a topic that some churches may find uncomfortable or challenging to address. Yet, the Gospels provide multiple accounts of Jesus healing those possessed by demons, indicating that this was a significant part of His ministry. If Jesus cared deeply for those who were beleaguered by demonic forces, then we should too. While not everyone may feel called to engage directly in this type of spiritual warfare, we are all called to pray for those who are bound by demonic forces, as well as for those who fight for their deliverance.

Reflections

How does the story of the boy with epilepsy challenge your understanding of faith in spiritual warfare?

In what ways can you incorporate prayer and fasting into your spiritual discipline, especially when faced with significant challenges?

How can you support those who are called to engage in spiritual warfare, even if you don't feel directly called to it?

....
....
....
....
....
....
....
....

From Status to Servanthood

"The best way to find yourself is to lose yourself in the service of others." - Mahatma Gandhi

43. Reading: Matthew 18:1-5

Today, if we were asked, "What's your status?' we might think about relationship status, job status, financial status – the list is endless. The word 'status' refers to our position in relation to someone else. If we're honest, when we're asking someone status-related questions, we're usually trying to decide how we rank in relation to them. We'll be happy to know the disciples were no different. Matthew 18 opens with the disciples wanting to clarify, "Who, then, is the greatest in the kingdom of heaven?" (Matthew 18:1). Jesus has been teaching and modelling humility, but they want to know who will hold the number one position in the Kingdom!

Here are two comments on the text:

"They doubtless fancied a temporal kingdom of the Messiah, in which places would be bestowed." (Matthew Poole)

"They dreamt of a distribution of honours and offices, a worldly monarchy, like the kingdoms of the earth." (John Trapp)

The disciples' question shows their misunderstanding of Jesus' mission. While Jesus was preparing to endure the most humiliating and painful death imaginable, His followers were concerned about their status. They were likely surprised by Jesus' response: "Unless you change and become like little children, you will never enter the kingdom of heaven" (Matthew 18:3). In the cultural context of that time, children were seen as vulnerable and without status or power. Jesus was emphasising the importance of humility and complete dependence on God instead of striving for greatness or recognition.

Jesus set aside His own will for the sake of God's will, teaching us that true greatness in the kingdom of heaven is found in humility and self-denial.

Reflections

What aspects of your life are driven by a desire for status or recognition?

How does striving for status impact your relationship with God and others?

What practical steps can you take to cultivate humility and a childlike trust in God?

....
....
....
....
....
....
....

Chasing the One

"The shepherd always tries to persuade the sheep that their interests and his own are the same." - Stendhal

44. Reading: Matthew 18:10-14

In our last reading we saw the disciples come to Jesus with a question: "Who then is greatest in the kingdom of heaven?" Jesus responds by drawing their attention to the value of humility and of care for those who may seem insignificant or vulnerable. This passage includes the well-known parable of the lost sheep, where Jesus tells of a shepherd who leaves 99 sheep to go in search of the one that has gone astray. The shepherd's actions reveal God's heart – the relentless pursuit of every individual, no matter how far they have wandered.

The parable beautifully illustrates the nature of God's love. Just as a shepherd wouldn't rest until the lost sheep was found, God will not give up on us, no matter how lost we might be. Jesus' words remind us that each of us holds immense worth in God's eyes, so much so that He will go to great lengths to bring us back into His fold.

This relentless pursuit of the lost is reminiscent of a scene from the film *Taken*, where Liam Neeson's character vows to do whatever it takes to rescue his kidnapped daughter. During a phone call, he tells the kidnappers, "I will look for you, I will find you, and I will kill you." In a similar but even more profound way, Jesus, the Good Shepherd, will stop at nothing to seek and save those who are lost. The parable reassures us of God's unwavering commitment to our salvation. It is not His will for any of us to perish (Matthew 18:14). God's love is so deep that He will leave the 99 just to find the one.

This passage invites us to reflect on the value God places on each person and challenges us to see others through that same lens. It also reassures us that no matter how far we may have strayed, God is always searching for us, ready to bring us back into His loving embrace.

Reflections

How do you view yourself in relation to God's pursuit? Do you feel like the one sheep He would leave the 99 to find?

In what ways can you mirror God's love for the lost in your own life?

How does this parable challenge your understanding of worthiness and significance in the kingdom of heaven?

Practical Task

This week, take time to reach out to someone who may feel overlooked or insignificant. Let them know that they are valued and seen, just as God values and sees each one of us.

....
....
....
....
....

Privacy First

"... if your brother sins against you, go and tell him his fault between you and him alone. That is the rule." - C.S. Lewis

45. Reading: Matthew 18:15-17

*C*onflict is an inevitable part of human relationships, even within the church. In Matthew 18:15-17, Jesus provides a clear and compassionate guide for addressing situations where a fellow believer sins against us. This passage offers a blueprint not only for resolving disputes but also for restoring relationships within the Christian community.

Jesus begins by instructing us to approach the person privately to discuss the issue one-on-one. Ideally, the situation can be resolved at this stage: The other person listens and acknowledges their wrongdoing, reconciliation is achieved, and you have "gained your brother" (Matthew 18:15). In our culture, where everything is posted online, Jesus' instructions to deal with wrongs privately is especially wise. This initial step highlights the value of addressing issues directly rather than resorting to gossip or public shaming. Reconciliation, not retribution, is God's desire for His people.

However, if the other person refuses to listen, Jesus advises escalating the matter by involving one or two others. This step is rooted in the Jewish legal principle found in Deuteronomy 19:15, which emphasises the need for multiple witnesses to establish the truth. The additional people not only serve as witnesses but also bring different perspectives that might help the offender see their error and turn back.

If the person we are at odds with still refuses to repent, the matter should be brought before the church. At that point, Jesus says, "... if he refuses to listen even to the church, treat him as you would a heathen or a tax collector" (Matthew 18:17). For Jesus' audience, this would have carried significant weight. However, it's important to remember that Jesus, who Himself called a tax collector to be His disciple, isn't advocating for shunning the individual. Rather, He is recognising that they need to be won back to the faith.

This process is infused with grace at every step, reflecting God's relentless pursuit of reconciliation and restoration. It echoes the parable of the lost sheep we examined yesterday, where the shepherd leaves the 99 to seek out the one that has gone astray. Jesus' approach is in direct opposition to today's cancel culture, which often thrives on public shaming and offers little room for forgiveness. Instead, Jesus models a way of dealing with conflict that values privacy, has a process, and offers repeated opportunities for repentance.

However, Jesus' method is not without boundaries. Persistent unrepentance cannot be tolerated, as it poses a risk to the spiritual health of the church. As believers, we must also be vigilant in seeking God's guidance to reveal our own sins, allowing Him to work in our hearts privately before our sins are exposed publicly.

Reflections

How do you typically handle conflict with others? Do you tend to address issues directly, or do you avoid confrontation?

How does Jesus' approach to conflict resolution challenge the way you think about dealing with disputes within the church?

In what ways can you apply the principles of grace and reconciliation in your interactions with others, especially in situations of conflict?

Practical Task

This week, consider if there is someone with whom you have unresolved conflict. Take the first step towards reconciliation by approaching them privately in a spirit of humility and grace, following the model that Jesus laid out. Pray for wisdom and guidance before initiating the conversation, asking God to work in both of your hearts for a peaceful resolution.

The Infinite Call to Forgiveness

"To be a Christian means to forgive the inexcusable because God has forgiven the inexcusable in you." - C.S. Lewis

46. Reading: Matthew 18:21-22

Love and forgiveness are two closely intertwined themes that run throughout the Bible and are most powerfully displayed on the Cross. From the moment Adam and Eve sinned, humanity needed forgiveness and a Saviour. God's boundless love drove Him to send Jesus to the Cross, bearing the cost for our forgiveness.

In today's reading, Peter asks Jesus a question that many of us have pondered: "Lord, how often should I forgive someone who sins against me? Seven times?" (Matthew 18:21). Peter likely suggested seven times because of his understanding of Jewish teachings, which suggested that forgiving someone three times was sufficient.

However, Jesus, as He often does, takes Peter's suggestion and magnifies it beyond human expectations. Jesus responds, "I tell you, not seven times, but 77 times" (or "70 times seven" in some translations). The call here isn't literally for 490 instances of forgiveness; instead, Jesus is emphasising that forgiveness should be limitless. It's not about keeping a tally; it's about living in a state of continuous grace, just as God continuously forgives us.

Here Michael J. Wilkins in the *NIV Application Commentary* accurately sums it up:

"Jesus' response to Peter's question indicates that Peter does not think broadly enough about the nature of forgiveness in the kingdom community. As magnanimous as Peter might view his allowance of forgiveness (seven times), Jesus is conceiving of forgiveness in much more expansive terms. The number 'seven' and its variations connote fullness or perfection, so Jesus' use of these numbers implies that unlimited forgiveness characterizes the kingdom. Moreover, the use of 'seven' and 'seventy-seven' evokes Genesis 4:24: 'If Cain is avenged seven times, then Lamech seventy-seven times.' This allusion signals a reversal based on the coming kingdom. As unlimited revenge characterized the entry of sin into human existence, so the restoration of God's ways and God's kingdom brings the possibility of unlimited forgiveness."

Forgiveness is challenging, especially when someone has deliberately hurt us or refuses to acknowledge their wrongdoing. However, it's important to remember that forgiveness is more about freeing the person who has been wronged than the perpetrator. The freedom that comes from forgiving others is a reflection of the forgiveness that we receive from God.

Jesus illustrates this concept further with the parable of the unforgiving servant (Matthew 18:23-35). In this story, a servant is forgiven an enormous debt by his master, yet he refuses to forgive a much smaller debt owed to him by another servant. The parable demonstrates the importance of forgiveness in our lives as Christians – we must aim to forgive others as we have been forgiven.

Reflections

How do you feel when you are wronged by someone? Do you find it difficult to forgive?

In what ways can you remind yourself of the infinite forgiveness God extends to you when you struggle to forgive others?

How can you cultivate a heart of forgiveness that reflects God's love in your daily interactions?

Practical Task

This week, take a moment to think of someone you may be holding a grudge against or have yet to forgive. Pray for God to soften your heart and to help you take a step towards forgiveness, whether it's through prayer, a kind gesture, or a conversation. Remember, forgiveness is a journey, not a one-time event.

....
....
....
....
....
....
....
....

Bringing the Next Generation to Jesus

"Children are the hands by which
we take hold of heaven."
- Henry Ward Beecher

47. Reading: Matthew 19:13-15

Jesus uses children in this passage to continue teaching His disciples that God's reign concerns itself with those who have lowly social status such as children, women, and the poor; it is safeguarding them that the disciples should be focussed on, not who will be the greatest in heaven. However, we can also extract some practical wisdom about the value of children in the kingdom of God and parental responsibility. Children are among God's greatest gifts, and with that gift comes responsibility. As parents, guardians, or even mentors, our role isn't just to provide for physical needs – love, food, and shelter – but to ensure spiritual growth. In Matthew 19:13-15, we see a beautiful demonstration of this when parents bring their children to Jesus. They recognise something we, too, must understand: Jesus' touch and blessing are vital for their children's future.

The passage shows the disciples rebuking the parents, likely because they misunderstood Jesus' mission and underestimated the importance of children in God's eyes. However, Jesus corrects them with an important lesson: "Let the little children come to Me, and do not forbid them; for of such is the kingdom of heaven" (Matthew 19:14). Jesus' response teaches us that children are precious to God and introducing them to Him early is crucial.

The parents in this story didn't wait until their children were older to bring them to Jesus; they seized the moment while their children were still young. This aligns with Proverbs 22:6, which says, "Train up a child in the way he should go, and when he is old he will not depart from it." Parents have a small but powerful window to instil a love for God, which can guide their children as they grow.

Whether we're parents, grandparents, aunts, uncles, or teachers, we all have an opportunity to bring children to Jesus through our influence. Even if we aren't parents, our prayers can have a powerful impact. Jesus laid His hands on the children and prayed for them, reminding us that prayer is one of the most effective ways we can care for the children in our lives.

Reflections

How does Jesus' response to the children challenge your view of children and their importance in the kingdom of God?

If you're a parent or mentor, how can you more actively introduce the children you care for to Jesus in your daily life?

For those without children, how can you influence the next generation through your prayers or actions?

Practical Task

This week, take time to pray for the children in your life, whether they are your own or children you know. Consider practical ways to share God's love with them – through a Bible story, a prayer, or simply leading by example.

An Invitation to True Freedom

"The greatest enemy of our freedom is not the things we don't have, but the things we have that make us think we don't need Jesus." - John Piper

48. Reading: Matthew 19:16-22

*I*n essence, the Ten Commandments are about fostering good relationships. The first four commandments focus on our relationship with God, while the remaining six guide our interactions with others. These commandments are not merely a list of restrictions; they provide a framework for living in liberty and keeping right relations. When the rich young ruler approaches Jesus in Matthew 19, he appears to have it all – wealth, status, and confidence in his moral goodness. Yet, after his encounter with Jesus, he leaves with a heavy heart, "sorrowful" (Matthew 19:22).

The young ruler's question is a good one: "What must I do to have eternal life?" Interestingly, Jesus responds by telling him to keep the commandments, but He doesn't mention eternal life specifically. Instead, Jesus says to keep the commandments "If you want to enter into life." This response suggests that while the commandments cannot save us, they guide us into a life of flourishing with God and others.

Jesus then addresses the root of the young man's issue. He lists several commandments but omits the one about coveting. Instead, Jesus quotes Leviticus 19:18: "Love your neighbour as yourself," a commandment the young man would have known well. The young man confidently asserts that he has kept all these, but Jesus exposes the deeper issue: "If you want to be perfect, go and sell all your possessions and give the money to the poor, and you will have treasure in heaven. Then come, follow me" (Matthew 19:21).

The word 'perfect' here, from the Greek telios, means complete or whole, suggesting that the young man's spiritual journey is incomplete. His wealth has become his idol, something he loves more than God. Jesus invites him to find true completeness by letting go of what he cherishes most.

One of the most poignant moments in Scripture occurs in Matthew 19:22 (NLT): "But when the young man heard this, he went away sad, for he had many possessions." The young man remains nameless, an anonymity that invites us to see ourselves in his story and examine our own idols. Unlike the rich young ruler, we are called to make a different choice – to surrender our idols and follow Jesus fully.

Reflections

What are the idols in your life that you struggle to surrender to God?

How do the Ten Commandments guide you in your relationships with God and others?

What does true perfection or completeness in Christ look like for you personally?

Practical Task

Identify one possession or pursuit that may be taking priority over your relationship with God. This week, take a tangible step to lessen its hold on your life – whether that means giving something away, reducing time spent on it, or redirecting your focus towards God.

....
....
....
....
....
....
....
....
....
....
....
....
....
....
....
....
....
....

The Power of Context

"Context is everything; it shapes our understanding and guides our actions." - Anonymous

49. Reading: Matthew 19:23-26

$\mathcal{S}$cripture is best grasped when we understand the context in which it was written. The well-known verse, "With God all things are possible" (Matthew 19:26), is often quoted to express the belief that nothing is beyond God's power. While this is true, knowing the verse's original context can deepen our understanding of it. This statement is derived from a conversation between Jesus and His disciples after Jesus' encountered a rich young ruler. In the wake of this conversation, Jesus remarked that it is easier for a camel to go through the eye of a needle than for a rich person to enter the kingdom of God. The disciples were astonished and asked, "Who then can be saved?" Jesus' response, "With men this is impossible, but with God all things are possible," is a powerful reminder that salvation – something utterly impossible for us to achieve on our own – is made possible by God's grace.

It's also helpful to understand the cultural landscape in which the verse sits. When Jesus says, "…it is easier for a camel to go through the eye of a needle than for a rich man to enter the kingdom…" (Matthew 19:24), His words would have been at odds with the Jewish belief that a person's wealth was linked to God's blessings. The presumption would have been if you were Jewish and rich you had God's favour, and, therefore, entry into heaven should have been almost certainly assured. The astonishment and subsequent question from the disciples in verse 25, "…who then can be saved?" makes more sense knowing this context. Jesus' hyperbole would have made them think. It also demonstrates that every word and example used by Jesus is used with intention.

Digging deeper into God's Word can feel challenging, but it is in these moments of exploration that we uncover the richness of God's truth. Each passage and each word is intentionally placed, not just for the audience of its time but for us today. Understanding the context of Jesus' words about wealth, salvation, and God's grace in Matthew 19 allows us to see that salvation isn't something we can earn through our efforts or wealth – it's a gift of God's grace. Our lives can transform when we grasp not just the words on the page but the circumstances in which they were spoken, allowing us to share a more complete picture of God's heart with others.

Reflections

How can understanding the historical and cultural context of a scripture change the way you apply it to your life today?

Have you ever been challenged or surprised by a passage when you understood it in its full context? What did that teach you?

....
....
....
....
....
....

Kingdom Culture: A Reversal

"In the kingdom of God, the first are last and the last are first. Those who humble themselves in service will be exalted, and those who try to exalt themselves will be humbled. The gospel turns the world's values upside down."
- Timothy Keller

50. Reading: Matthew 19:27-30

Peter's question to Jesus, "See, we have left all and followed You. Therefore what shall we have?" (Matthew 19:27), ties into the theme of status discussed in our previous readings. Peter is genuinely concerned: If a rich man can't easily enter the Kingdom of Heaven, what will the disciples get for following Jesus? This kind of thinking isn't too far from our own culture's mindset of "What's in it for me?" On the one hand, this is understandable – we work, and we expect to get paid. However, Jesus is challenging His disciples' – and the Jewish culture's – view of status and reward.

If we carefully examine what Jesus says about those who follow Him, there is no mention of earthly riches. Instead, He speaks of the disciples sitting on 12 thrones to judge the 12 tribes of Israel (verse 28) and promises that those who have given up much for His sake will receive it back a hundredfold and inherit eternal life (verse 29). A hundredfold in this context does not refer to material wealth but to God's immense blessings, which far outweigh any sacrifice. At the heart of it, the ultimate reward for following Jesus is His presence.

Finally, Jesus emphasises the idea that those who are seen as lowly or insignificant will be prioritised in God's Kingdom. He says, "But many who are first will be last, and the last first" (Matthew 19:30). Without giving too much away, this theme of the last being first perfectly transitions into the parable Jesus shares in Matthew 20 – it's a continuation of His teaching on the Kingdom's values.

The kingdom of God was a reversal of Jewish cultural expectations. These truths Jesus spoke would have been perplexing and difficult to digest. We have the benefit of their experience, and yet, even for us, living out these radical values is challenging. However, through the power of the Holy Spirit, it is possible for us to live lives that elevate those who are deemed to have lowly status and to temper our own self-interest.

Reflections

In what ways do you find yourself asking, "What's in it for me?" when it comes to following Jesus?

How does Jesus' promise of a hundredfold reward challenge your understanding of what it means to be blessed?

Are there areas in your life where you struggle to prioritise the values of God's Kingdom over cultural values?

How can you actively look out for and care for those who might be seen as 'low status' in your community?

....

....

....

....

A Generous God

"You cannot empty God's treasury. There is no end to His generosity."
- Charles Spurgeon

51. Reading: Matthew 20:1-16

*I*f there's a chapter of the Bible that challenges our ideas of equality, it's Matthew 20. Jesus begins this powerful teaching with a statement in Matthew 19:30, "But many who are first will be last, and the last first." It is from this lens that Jesus offers us the parable that completely redefines the idea of fairness and reward in the kingdom of God.

The story Jesus shares is about a landowner who hires workers throughout the day – some at dawn, some at the third and sixth hours, and others as late as the eleventh hour. This detail of the eleventh hour is key. In ancient times, the workday was from 6 a.m. to 6 p.m., divided into 12 hours. So, when the landowner hires workers at the eleventh hour – around 5 p.m. – they have only one hour left to work.

When it comes time to pay the workers, the landowner begins with those hired last. To everyone's surprise, they receive a full day's wage – the same as those who worked from the early morning. Naturally, the early workers expect more, but they receive exactly what they were promised. Outraged, they argue, but the landowner reminds them that he has given them what was agreed, and that he is free to be generous with what is his.

In today's culture, we might expect this situation to hit the headlines, with people questioning the equitability of such an act. But what was Jesus really trying to teach us?

God's Generosity

First and foremost, this parable shows us the depth of God's generosity. Like the landowner, God is always reaching out to bring more people into His kingdom. It's not about how long we've been Christians or how much we've done for God – His mercy and promise of eternal life are based solely on His love and grace. The reward of eternal life is the same for someone who has known Christ for decades as it is for someone who has come to know Him only moments before their death.

Grace vs. Human Merit

The landowner's decision to pay all the workers equally, regardless of how long they worked, emphasises that God's grace is not based on our efforts. Our good works don't earn us more grace or favour with God. Grace is a gift, unearned and freely given. God blesses according to His will, not by our expectations of fairness.

Equality in the Kingdom of God

This parable also highlights the equality found in the kingdom of God. Jesus is teaching that, in God's eyes, we are all equal regardless of when we come to faith. One powerful example is the thief on the cross who, in his final moments, accepts Jesus and is promised eternal life (Luke 23:39-43). This shows that our timeline in accepting Christ doesn't determine our reward in heaven – God's grace does.

For many of us, this parable challenges our sense of equitability. We often want to see rewards that correspond with effort. But Jesus is reminding us that God's ways are not like ours. He calls us to trust in His generosity, rather than in our sense of what we deserve.

Reflections

When do you find yourself comparing your efforts to those of others, especially in your spiritual life?

How does this parable challenge your understanding of equality in God's Kingdom?

Are there areas in your life where you've struggled to celebrate God's grace in the lives of others?

....
....
....
....
....
....
....
....
....
....
....
....

Specificity

"We are too vague in our prayers. Be definite with God. Tell Him exactly what you want, for He knows what you need, but He delights in hearing you ask for it." - Charles Spurgeon

52. Reading: Matthew 20:29-34

*I*n Matthew 20:29-34, we find a powerful story, one wherein Jesus heals two blind men. These men are sitting by the roadside when they hear that Jesus is passing by. Without hesitation, they cry out, "Have mercy on us, O Lord, Son of David!" (Matthew 20:30). Their call reveals two things: First, they recognise who Jesus is, and second, they believe He is capable of healing them. Their persistence highlights their faith – they know this might be their only chance to regain their sight.

Interestingly, despite their loud pleas, the crowd tries to silence them. But these men are not discouraged. Instead, they cry out even louder. This act of determination captures Jesus' attention, and He stops to ask them a question that might seem odd at first: "What do you want Me to do for you?" (Matthew 20:32).

Why would Jesus ask this question? Surely it was obvious that these blind men wanted their sight restored. Yet, their initial cry for mercy was general. Jesus' question teaches us something crucial: God desires that we be specific in our requests.

The question, "What do you want?" asks us to state our hopes. Although God knows our needs before we ask (Matthew 6:8), being specific in our prayers helps us clarify what we truly seek and determine whether it aligns with God's will. Vague prayers can leave us uncertain when answers come, whereas precise requests allow us to recognise God's hand in our lives more clearly.

Additionally, specific prayers help us to assess whether what we're asking for is truly aligned with Scripture and God's plan for us. By focusing our requests, we deepen our understanding of our desires and how they fit within God's broader purpose for our lives.

Jesus did heal the two blind men, but this story isn't just about a physical miracle – it's a lesson on persistence, faith, and the importance of praying with clear intent. Sometimes, God waits for us to be specific, not because He doesn't know what we need, but because it draws us closer to Him and strengthens our faith.

Reflections

Are there areas of your life where you've been praying general prayers? How can you make those requests more specific?

How can you ensure your prayers align with God's word and His will for your life?

How might being more specific in your prayers lead to greater awareness of how God answers them?

Practical Task

Take a moment to reflect on one key prayer request you've had recently. Spend time thinking about how you can make that request more specific and intentional. Write it down and align it with a relevant Bible verse, praying it daily this week.

Fickle Follower or Faithful Disciple?

"The crowd that cried 'Hosanna!' to Jesus on Palm Sunday was the same crowd that cried 'Crucify Him!' just a few days later. Human praise is fickle, but divine love is constant." - A.W. Tozer

53. Reading: Matthew 21:1-11

*I*n these verses, we witness Jesus' entry into Jerusalem, often referred to as the Triumphal Entry. The scene is set with great enthusiasm and celebration, as Jesus rides in on a donkey, fulfilling the prophecy from Zechariah 9:9. The crowd goes wild, laying down their cloaks and branches before Him, shouting, "Hosanna to the Son of David! Blessed is He who comes in the name of the Lord!" (Matthew 21:9).

It feels like a celebrity moment – Jesus is treated like a king, a superstar. The people are ecstatic, recognising Him as a prophet, a miracle worker, and the Messiah. It's a public display of praise and adoration that we might liken to modern-day fans cheering for their hero at a stadium or on a red carpet. But there's more brewing beneath the surface.

While it appears to be a moment of great honour for Jesus, we know the full story: Within a week, this same crowd will vanish. Jesus, who was welcomed with such excitement, will be hanging on a cross, abandoned by many of those who celebrated His arrival. The cheers of 'Hosanna' will fade into silence, and later, some will even join in the calls for His crucifixion.

This passage challenges us to reflect on how we view Jesus. Are we similar to the crowd, eager to praise Him when everything is going well, when our prayers are answered, and when there is no cost to pay for following Him?

Jesus' Triumphal Entry is a powerful reminder of the fickleness of human praise. When Jesus was healing the sick, feeding the multitudes, and performing miracles, the crowds were happy to follow Him. But when His path led to the Cross, the crowd's enthusiasm disappeared.

As Christians, we must guard against spiritual amnesia. It's easy to praise Jesus when life is comfortable, but what happens when following Him comes at a cost? The crowds shouted, 'Hosanna' because they expected a conquering king who would overthrow Roman oppression; instead, Jesus came as the suffering servant who would lay down His life. Would we have behaved any differently than the members of the crowd? The challenge for us is to move beyond the crowd's fleeting excitement and become faithful disciples who follow Jesus, not just in moments of celebration, but through every trial and challenge.

Reflections

Who is Jesus to you? Is He just someone who answers your prayers, or is He truly Lord and Saviour, even when life doesn't go as planned?

How does this passage challenge your heart? Are you quick to celebrate Jesus in public when it's easy, but hesitant when following Him might cost you something?

Handling Difficult People

"Conflict is inevitable, but combat is optional." - Max Lucado

54. Reading: Matthew 21:23-27

Jesus often faced difficult people, especially the religious leaders who constantly tried to trap Him. This passage is a typical example: The chief priests and elders confront Jesus with what seems like a reasonable question, but their real intent is to undermine Him. Instead of falling into their trap, Jesus asks them a question of His own, exposing their hypocrisy and forcing them to back down.

We can all relate to encountering difficult people in our lives – whether it's in the workplace, in our families, or at church. These are people who ask questions not to understand, but to manipulate or find fault. What's brilliant about Jesus' response is His wisdom and discernment. He doesn't feel pressured to answer directly or defend Himself. Instead, He responds with a question that reveals their motives and deflects the conflict.

This passage offers us three key lessons for dealing with difficult people:

Discernment and Wisdom

Jesus doesn't immediately answer His enemies. He takes control of the situation by asking a question in return. This is a reminder that we don't need to feel compelled to answer every question or accusation, especially when we sense it comes from a place of bad intent. It's okay to pause, reflect, and seek God's wisdom before responding. James 1:5 tells us, "If any of you lacks wisdom, you should ask God, who gives generously to all without finding fault, and it will be given to you."

We're Not Obliged to Respond on Someone Else's Terms

Jesus shows us that it's perfectly fine not to give an answer on the spot. Sometimes, people use questions as a way to exert pressure or control. Instead of getting caught in their game, we can, like Jesus, take a step back. We can respond with, "Let me think about that," or "I'm not going to answer that right now." This helps us avoid giving answers that we may later regret.

A Measured Approach to Conflict

Jesus' handling of this confrontation is calm, thoughtful, and wise. He doesn't lash out or try to forcefully prove His authority. Instead, He remains composed and in control, setting an example for how we should approach conflict. By staying calm and asking the right questions, we can often de-escalate situations and keep our integrity intact.

Reflections

How do you usually react to difficult or confrontational people? How can you apply Jesus' wisdom in those moments?

Are there any situations where you've felt pressured to respond hastily? How could you handle them differently next time?

Practical Task

This week, if you encounter a challenging person or situation, pause and ask God for wisdom before responding. Practise the art of asking questions instead of giving immediate answers to avoid being drawn into conflict.

The Chosen

"God's invitation to salvation is open to all, but it is only through the response of faith that one is chosen. Many are called, but few are willing to come."
- John MacArthur

55. Reading: Matthew 22:1-14

There's a popular series called *The Chosen* that explores the lives of those who followed Jesus. The title also resonates deeply with today's passage. In the parable of the wedding feast, Jesus tells the story of a king who invites many guests to the wedding of his son. But those initially invited either ignore the invitation, go about their own business, or worse – mistreat and kill the king's servants. In response, the king invites people from the highways – both good and bad – to fill the wedding hall.

When the king later notices a guest without a wedding garment, he confronts him. The guest is speechless and is thrown out into darkness. The parable ends with Jesus saying, "For many are called, but few are chosen." This is a powerful lesson about accepting God's invitation and being spiritually prepared for eternity.

Three Key Lessons

1. **God's Invitation Is for All, but Acceptance Is Our Choice:** In the parable, the king's invitation represents God's offer of eternal life. Just like the original guests, we all have the freedom to accept or reject God's offer. Sadly, many are indifferent to this invitation or distracted by worldly concerns. This is a sobering reminder that while God calls everyone, He doesn't force anyone to respond.

2. **We Must Be Spiritually Ready:** The guest without the proper wedding garment symbolises someone trying to enter heaven on their own terms. We cannot stand before God clothed in our own righteousness. Our 'garments' – the outward signs of our lives and choices – must be washed clean by Jesus. This speaks of the need for a transformed life, made possible through Christ's sacrifice.
3. **There Are No Excuses:** The guest who was thrown out was speechless. This shows that when we stand before God, we can offer no excuse if we haven't accepted His gift of salvation. This is a clear call for us to take our faith seriously and be prepared for the consequences of rejecting or neglecting it.

This parable is a serious reminder that while God's invitation is generous and open to all, it requires a response from us. Simply being called is not enough; we must embrace the transformation that comes with following Jesus.

Reflections

Do your daily choices reflect someone who has accepted God's invitation of eternal life?

Why is it not enough to rely on our own goodness or efforts to enter heaven?

What can you do to ensure you're spiritually ready, clothed in the righteousness of Christ?

The Love Triangle

"To love God with all your heart, soul, and mind is not a mere emotional or intellectual exercise; it is a comprehensive, life-encompassing commitment that shapes every part of you." - Dallas Willard

56. Reading: Matthew 22:34-40

After the sharing of the parable of the wedding feast, the Pharisees attempt to trap Jesus with a tricky question about paying taxes. On the same day, the Sadducees – who deny the resurrection – also try to ensnare Him, but Jesus skilfully silences them. When the Pharisees hear that Jesus has silenced the Sadducees, they regroup and test Him again by asking, "Which is the greatest commandment in the Law?" Jesus, perceiving their intentions, turns the moment into a powerful lesson on love, providing us with essential guidance on our relationship with God, ourselves, and others.

Jesus begins by instructing us to love God with all our heart, soul, and mind. The reference to these three aspects of our being is deliberate. Love is not just an emotional whim or a fleeting feeling; it's a profound, intentional commitment that engages our entire being – our emotions, intellect, and spiritual essence.

Next, Jesus outlines the proper way to order the love in our lives. It's a divine hierarchy that, if disrupted, can lead to disorder and disharmony. We must love God first. If we place anyone or anything above God, it becomes an idol, and we lose the ability to love others properly. The world's notion of self-love is, in fact, a distorted version of God's original design. God never intended for us to walk through life burdened by self-loathing. Instead, He calls us to love ourselves, but in proper measure – just as we love others.

Notice the order: God first, then ourselves, and finally, others, with the same degree of care and love that we show ourselves. We are called to love upwards – placing God first – then inwards, nurturing a healthy love for ourselves, and, out of that abundance, we can love others well.

Reflections

What does it mean to you to love God with all your heart, soul, and mind?

In what ways might you have placed someone or something above God in your life?

How can understanding the correct hierarchy for love bring more harmony into your relationships?

Practical Task

This week, spend time each day reflecting on one aspect of your love for God, yourself, and others. Ask God to reveal any areas where your love might be out of order, and seek His guidance on how to realign it according to His will.

....
....
....
....
....

A Call to Self-Examination

"An unexamined life is not worth living." - Socrates

57. Reading: Matthew 23

Matthew 23 is a sobering chapter that highlights the consequences of rejecting Jesus. This passage marks the final days before the religious leaders – who have consistently opposed Jesus – convince Rome to crucify Him. By this point, Jesus has silenced their challenges, leaving them unable to refute His wisdom or moral authority. Their only remaining recourse is to plot His death, which they will soon do.

In many Bibles, this chapter is titled, "Woe to the Scribes and Pharisees," a fitting description of Jesus' powerful denunciation of these religious leaders. Their false teachings have led people into spiritual darkness, and Jesus' rebuke is sharp and unyielding. His righteous anger is evident, but so is His deep sorrow. The chapter culminates in Jesus lamenting over Jerusalem, heartbroken by its unwillingness to turn to Him.

It's easy to read this chapter and feel a sense of superiority, thinking that we are not like the scribes and Pharisees. But the reality is, whenever we choose to live by our own rules or assume we know better than God, we fall into the same trap. Every day, we must examine our hearts to ensure that the rebukes Jesus delivered do not apply to us.

Reflections

Which of the woes mentioned in Matthew 23 surprised or impacted you the most?

In what ways might you be behaving like the scribes and Pharisees, perhaps without realising it?

How can you align your life more closely with Jesus' teachings and avoid the pitfalls of hypocrisy?

Practical Task

Take time this week to reflect on each of the woes in Matthew 23. Ask God to reveal any areas in your life where you may be falling into patterns like those of the scribes and Pharisees. Write down what He shows you and make a plan for how you can change course, seeking His help in prayer.

....
....
....
....
....
....
....
....
....

Suffering Well

Suffering is not a meaningless interruption in God's plan. It is an essential part of His sovereign design for bringing about the joy of His people and the spread of His gospel."
- John Piper

58. Reading: Matthew 24:1-14

We all long for lives filled with happiness, free from pain and suffering. However, as followers of Jesus, we must come to terms with the reality that suffering is an inevitable part of our journey and learn how to suffer well. In Matthew 24:13, Jesus says, "But he who endures to the end shall be saved." One definition for the word 'endures' is to suffer something painful patiently. The call to endure is central to our faith. Yet, suffering well isn't the kind of message that draws crowds to church. It's challenging, uncomfortable, and far from the feel-good teachings we often prefer.

In Matthew 24, Jesus speaks to His disciples about the trials that lie ahead. At this point, they still haven't fully grasped that He is about to face the ultimate suffering on the Cross. Jesus will willingly submit to the Roman authorities, influenced by Jewish leaders, and endure a death that is intended as a punishment for criminals. Despite the unimaginable pain, He won't murmur or complain when the nails pierce His hands and feet. He won't retaliate when they mock and abuse Him. Jesus will suffer well, setting an example for us on how to endure suffering with grace and patience.

The Christian journey is not without its trials. We need only to look at the story of Job or Joseph or reflect on our own lives, which are filled with moments of pain and hardship. It's easy to compare ourselves to others and fall into self-pity when we're in the midst of suffering. But when we consider what Jesus endured on the Cross, it should shift our perspective. We see that enduring suffering is not about avoiding pain but about holding fast to our faith through it all.

Reflections

How does reflecting on Jesus' suffering on the Cross help you to endure your own trials?

In what areas of your life do you find it most challenging to suffer well?

What steps can you take to shift your perspective and embrace endurance in the face of hardship?

Practical Task

This week, whenever you encounter a difficult situation, take a moment to reflect on the Cross. Meditate on the suffering Jesus endured and ask Him to help you endure your own trials with patience and faith.

....
....
....
....
....

A Sense of Urgency

"Time is the most valuable thing a man can spend." - Theophrastus

59. Reading: Matthew 25:1-13

Are you someone who gets things done well in advance, or do you tend to procrastinate, leaving tasks until the last possible moment? Most of us fall into one of these two categories, with a few of us landing somewhere in between. This tension between preparation and procrastination is vividly portrayed in the parable of the wise and foolish virgins.

In this parable, one group of virgins prepared for the bridegroom's arrival in advance, while the other group delayed until the last minute, scrambling for oil as the bridegroom approached. This story is closely linked to Jesus' words in Matthew 24:36, where He explains that no one knows the day or hour of His return – not even the angels in heaven. The message is clear: We must live in a state of constant readiness.

When it comes to our spiritual lives, procrastination should not be an option. We can't afford to delay the work of character development, forgiveness, or any other area where God has been nudging us. Both sets of virgins knew the bridegroom was coming; the difference was that one group chose to prepare, while the other delayed. The consequences of their choices were eternal – when the foolish virgins tried to enter, they were turned away with the chilling words, "I do not know you."

This parable serves as a powerful reminder that our readiness isn't just about knowing Jesus is coming – it's about living each day as though He could return at any moment. The call to 'watch' is a call to active, ongoing preparation.

Reflections

Is there something God is asking you to do that you've been putting off? What's holding you back?

Do you see yourself more in the wise or foolish virgins, and why?

What additional insights or lessons do you glean from the parable of the wise and foolish virgins?

....
....
....
....
....
....
....
....
....
....
....

Does Your Faith Have a Price?

"The betrayal of Jesus by Judas teaches us about grace, forgiveness, and the cost of love." - Timothy Keller

60. Reading: Matthew 26:14-16

*B*etrayal is always painful, but it's especially devastating when it comes from someone we love and trust. Judas' betrayal of Jesus falls into this category, and it's made even more tragic by the fact that Judas put a price on his relationship with Jesus – 30 pieces of silver. In today's terms, this would be roughly £200 or $260, depending on the exchange rate. Despite witnessing countless miracles, hearing Jesus' teachings first-hand, and experiencing life with Jesus for nearly four years, Judas idolised and valued money more than his relationship.

It's sobering to realise that Judas was not a fictional character but a real person who walked with God in human flesh and still chose to betray Him for financial gain. This forces us to reflect on our own lives. Every time we refuse to deal with sin or allow idols to take root in our hearts, we are not so different from Judas. While we may not physically hand Jesus over in exchange for money, when we prioritise anything above our relationship with Him, we effectively say, "I am the god of my life."

The critical difference between us and Judas should be our response to the Holy Spirit's conviction. When we are confronted with our sin, we can repent – a chance that Judas tragically missed. Living in a fallen world means that we will sin, and there may even be times when we sin wilfully. However, we must never harden our hearts to the Holy Spirit's gentle plea for repentance. God's grace is always available, but we must choose to turn back to Him.

Reflections

Is there anything in your life that you've allowed to take precedence over your relationship with Jesus?

How do you respond when the Holy Spirit convicts you of sin? Do you resist, or do you repent?

What can you learn from Judas' story to safeguard your faith against similar pitfalls?

Practical Task

This week, take some quiet time to reflect on areas in your life where you may have placed something above your relationship with God. It could be a habit, an attitude, or even a desire. Ask the Holy Spirit to reveal these to you, and then take a step towards repentance, making a conscious decision to realign your priorities with God's will.

....
....
....
....
....

Grace Beyond Failure

"Grace means that all of your mistakes now serve a purpose instead of serving shame." - Brené Brown

61. Reading: Matthew 26:31-35

We may all know someone who shares traits similar to Peter's – boldness, confidence, fearlessness, honesty, and zealousness. While these qualities are admirable, they can sometimes lead to impulsiveness or self-reliance. In Matthew 26, we see Peter's boldness when Jesus forewarns His disciples that they will all fall away because of Him. Peter immediately denies this, declaring, "Even if all fall away on account of you, I never will" (v. 33). Yet we must not overlook verse 35: "And all the other disciples said the same."

While Peter's voice was the loudest, he was not alone in his conviction. All the disciples pledged their loyalty to Jesus, yet their resolve faltered when tested. This passage teaches us that strong convictions often reveal their true strength only under pressure. Without the Holy Spirit's power dwelling within us, we are no match for our own flesh or external temptations and pressures.

Peter genuinely believed he would never deny Jesus. The depth of his remorse after his denial (Matthew 26:75) reveals a heart that recognised its weakness and sought restoration through repentance. The most beautiful takeaway from Peter's denial is the assurance that there is always hope through repentance.

This narrative also highlights the heart of Jesus towards His disciples – and towards us. In His final hours, Jesus, facing His own suffering and death, focused on encouraging His followers. He warns them of their impending failures but also gives them hope: "But after I have risen, I will go ahead of you into Galilee" (Matthew 26:32).

These words would become a lifeline in the days following His crucifixion. They serve as a reminder of Jesus' unwavering faithfulness, even when we falter. We, too, have an even greater promise – that by placing our trust in Christ, we will spend eternity with Him.

Reflections

How can we cultivate humility and dependence on God instead of relying on ourselves?

What steps can we take to recognise and confront our spiritual weaknesses before they are tested?

How does Jesus' grace and forgiveness in the face of Peter's denial encourage us in our own moments of failure?

How does the promise of Christ's faithfulness inspire hope and perseverance in our daily walk?

....

....

....

....

The Wrestle

"Prayer does not change God,
but it changes him who prays."
- Søren Kierkegaard

62. Reading: Matthew 26:36-46

Today's reading from Gethsemane is one of the most profound moments in Jesus' earthly life. We witness the depth of His humanity and complete submission to the Father's will. The Cross looms, and Jesus knows that His mission is almost complete. All that remains is His death. If we fail to remember that Jesus is fully God and fully human, we might overlook the intense emotional struggle He experiences. In Gethsemane, we see Jesus, in His humanity, pleading with the Father. Three times, He asks for the cup of suffering to be taken from Him. This wasn't a casual prayer; it was a deep, agonising wrestle with the Father.

We learn that it's okay for us to wrestle with God when He asks us to do difficult things. When we feel out of control, uncertain, or insecure, God invites us to bring all our emotions to Him. He doesn't demand immediate, unfeeling submission; He wants our honesty, even when we're struggling.

In Matthew 26:45, after the third prayer, something shifts. Jesus returns to His disciples and says, "Behold, the hour is at hand…" After wrestling with God, Jesus faithfully accepts the Father's will for His life. This is a powerful reassurance for us. Submission to God's will doesn't always come easily or without struggle. For some, it might be a slow, reluctant journey; for others, it might be a bold step forward, grounded in past experiences of God's faithfulness.

Regardless of how we get there, as Christians, we must ultimately recognise and accept God's sovereignty over our lives.

Jesus' submission led to the salvation of the entire human race. While our submission might not have such a monumental impact, we can't underestimate what God can do through our obedience. No matter how small or insignificant it might seem, our willingness to submit to God's will has the potential to make a significant difference in the Kingdom.

Reflections

What is God asking you to do that you are currently wrestling with? What fears or concerns are holding you back from submitting?

Think back to times when God has asked you to submit to His will in the past. How did you feel during those times, and what were the outcomes? What do these experiences teach you about trusting God's plan?

Practical Task

This week, take some time to journal about an area where you are struggling to submit to God's will. Write down your fears, emotions, and thoughts honestly. Then, spend time in prayer, asking God to help you trust Him and to give you the strength to submit, even if the path ahead is challenging.

The Kiss of Betrayal

"Better an open enemy than a false friend." - Greek Proverb

63. Reading: Matthew 26:47-56

The moment had finally come. Judas, one of Jesus' chosen disciples, approached Him in Gethsemane with a kiss – the signal of betrayal. If this were a movie, we might find ourselves shouting at the screen, "Judas, don't do it!" However, the tragedy of this scene goes far beyond human emotion. Prophecy had foretold the betrayal and crucifixion of the Messiah, though Judas' name was not explicitly mentioned in any text. This ambiguity highlights a profound truth: Judas acted of his own will, yet his actions also fulfilled divine prophecy.

In John 13:27, we see an even deeper layer of this betrayal: "Now after the piece of bread, Satan entered him. Then Jesus said to him, 'What you do, do quickly.'" Judas had already set his heart on betrayal, and his decision opened the door for Satan to enter and solidify his course.

Lessons from Betrayal

This moment is laden with irony, sorrow, and spiritual significance. Judas' betrayal teaches us two key lessons:

1. **Betrayal Often Comes from Those Closest to Us**
   - Judas had walked with Jesus, witnessed His miracles, and been entrusted with ministry. Yet he handed Him over with a kiss – a gesture of affection

turned into a symbol of treachery. This reminds us that betrayal often comes from those we trust most deeply.
- Jesus' response, however, should be our model: He does not lash out or resist but submits to the Father's will. He even addresses Judas as "Friend" (v. 50), demonstrating love and compassion even in the face of ultimate betrayal.
- In our own lives, when we are betrayed or let down, Jesus challenges us to respond with grace, leaving justice and vengeance to God.

2. **God's Sovereignty in the Midst of Betrayal**
    - While Judas' actions were devastating, they were part of God's redemptive plan. This does not excuse Judas' choices, but it reveals a greater truth: God's sovereignty is not thwarted by human sin.
    - In moments of betrayal, we can trust that God is working all things for His glory and our ultimate good (Romans 8:28). Jesus endured the betrayal of Judas knowing it would lead to the Cross and, ultimately, the salvation of humankind.

Reflections

How do you typically react when you are betrayed or let down by someone close to you? How does Jesus' response challenge you?

Have you ever felt abandoned by people you relied on? How did that experience shape your faith and dependence on God?

Purity on Trial

"Jesus Christ did not just die for us; He died instead of us. He stood in our place, receiving the mockery, the beating, and the unjust condemnation that we deserved. His sacrifice was the ultimate demonstration of love and grace." - Tim Keller

64. Reading: Matthew 26:57-67

Jesus was brought before the Sanhedrin and subjected to what can only be described as a sham trial. This council of elite religious leaders, entrusted with upholding justice, sought false testimony to condemn Him. Yet, despite their efforts, no accusation could hold, for Jesus' life was blameless. His purity and integrity were undeniable, even under the harshest scrutiny.

This trial underscores a significant truth: Jesus is not merely an example of sinlessness; He is the perfect priest, fulfilling the divine vocation that humanity, through sin, could not. While it is remarkable that no fault was found in Him, the greater emphasis lies on His perfection as the Son of Man – the second Adam – who would fully realise humanity's calling to priesthood and righteousness.

The irony of this passage is profound: The earthly high priest and the Sanhedrin, who were supposed to represent God's justice, put the true heavenly High Priest on trial. When Jesus identifies Himself as the Son of Man (v. 64), He declares His unique role as the second Adam, the perfect fulfilment of humanity's priestly vocation. His trial foreshadows His ultimate work on the Cross, where He would secure righteousness for humanity.

This is the good news: Through Jesus, humanity has a perfect Saviour, who not only makes us righteous but also completes the work we cannot do on our own. Our perfection is not about living without fault but about trusting in the One who is faultless.

Reflections

How does understanding Jesus as the perfect High Priest change your perspective on your relationship with God?

What does it mean to you that Jesus not only makes us righteous but also completes the work that we cannot do on our own?

How does the irony of the earthly high priest judging the heavenly High Priest deepen your understanding of God's plan of redemption?

In what areas of your life do you need to trust more in the faultless work of Christ rather than striving for perfection on your own?

....
....
....
....
....
....
....
....
....

People Watchers

"Out of 100 men, one will read the Bible, the other 99 will read the Christian."
- D.L. Moody

65. Reading: Matthew 26:69-75

We're being watched, even when we don't realise it. Whether we're at work or simply going about our daily routines, people notice our actions, attitudes, and choices. With the rise of surveillance, this watchfulness is now our daily reality, and this therefore begs the question – when people look at our lives, what do they see? Would they recognise us as followers of Christ?

Peter found himself in this very position. As he sat in the courtyard, a servant girl approached him, declaring, "You also were with Jesus of Galilee" (Matthew 26:69). Peter had been recognised, not for anything he did in that moment, but simply because people had seen him with Jesus. Startled, he denied it. Then another servant girl said, "This fellow also was with Jesus of Nazareth" (Matthew 26:71). Peter denied it again, denying Jesus a second time.

Finally, those nearby remarked, "Surely you also are one of them, for your speech betrays you" (Matthew 26:73). John's account reveals that it was a relative of Malchus, the man whose ear Peter had cut off, who made this final accusation (John 18:26). In response, Peter swore an oath, vehemently denying that he knew Jesus. As the rooster crowed, Peter remembered Jesus' prophecy about his denials and walked away, overwhelmed with sorrow.

Peter's story is a reminder that our actions and words are on display. People see more than we think, and what they see has the power to either draw them closer to Christ or push them further away. We all get it wrong at times; we sin because we are human. We must accept that failure is part of our journey but should never become comfortable with sin in our lives.

Reflections

If someone were to watch the unfiltered version of your life for just 24 hours, would what they observe draw them to Christ?

When people see you, do they see someone who has been with Jesus?

How do fulfilled prophecies, like Jesus' words to Peter, strengthen your faith?

Practical Task

Reflect on a recent situation where your actions or words didn't align with your faith. Identify one specific change you can make this week to better reflect Christ in your daily interactions.

....
....
....
....
....
....

The Cost

"Sin may seem sweet in the moment, but it always carries a high price. It costs more than we can ever imagine, and ultimately, it costs the life of the Son of God." - R.C. Sproul

66. Reading: Matthew 27:3-10

One of the greatest lies of the enemy is convincing us that we can engage in sin or rebellion against God without facing any consequences. This deception first appeared in the Garden of Eden, when the serpent tricked Eve into eating the forbidden fruit, telling her she would not die but instead be like God (Genesis 3). We know how that turned out – not only for Eve, but for all of us. Even today, we live with the consequences of that choice.

Judas experienced this same deception. After betraying Jesus, he was filled with regret and tried to return the 30 pieces of silver, but the chief priests and elders had no interest in taking the money back – they had what they wanted: Jesus. In desperation, Judas threw the silver coins into the temple. Imagine the clatter of the coins as they scattered across the floor. Judas, overwhelmed by guilt and despair, left and tragically took his own life. What Judas thought would bring him happiness – money – ended up costing him his life. Similarly, Eve believed she would become like God, but instead, she lost her intimacy with God and succumbed to physical death as God had said.

Sin always has a cost. Jesus died on the Cross so we wouldn't have to pay the ultimate price, but that doesn't mean we're immune to the consequences of our actions in this life. When we choose to sin, there are always repercussions, even if they aren't immediately apparent. The temporary pleasure or gain we might seek can lead to long-term damage – whether it's broken relationships, lost trust, or missed opportunities for God's best in our lives.

Reflections

What lies have you believed about sin that have made it seem less costly than it truly is?

How have you experienced the hidden costs of sin in your own life or observed them in others?

In what ways can you remind yourself of the true consequences of sin before making choices?

Practical Task

This week, take time to reflect on an area of your life where you may be compromising or downplaying sin. Write down the potential costs of continuing in that behaviour, and ask God for the strength to choose His way instead.

....
....
....
....
....
....
....

Silence is Never Neutral

"Our lives begin to end the day we become silent about things that matter." - Martin Luther King Jr.

67. Reading: Matthew 27:11-26

*H*ave you ever found yourself in a situation where you knew something was wrong but lacked the moral courage to act? Pastor Martin Niemöller's poem "First They Came" captures the consequences of staying silent in the face of injustice. When we see wrongdoing and have the power to intervene but choose not to, we need to reflect on why we didn't speak up. Perhaps it was fear, embarrassment, or simply a desire to avoid conflict.

Pilate will forever be remembered as the man who washed his hands of his responsibility rather than standing up for what was right. Though we know from prophecy that Pilate couldn't have stopped the crucifixion of Jesus, like Judas, he had a choice in how he played his part in the story.

We can't take on every injustice we see, but there will be key moments in our lives when our voice could make a difference – or at least offer a different perspective. Sometimes it's as simple as not laughing at an unkind joke about a colleague, and, later, explaining privately why it was inappropriate. Other times, it might involve taking a more public stand or speaking up in uncomfortable settings.

Throughout His ministry, Jesus never shied away from confronting the injustice directly in His path. Consider the woman caught in adultery: While her accusers were ready to stone her, Jesus wrote in the ground, subtly reminding them of their own sins. Only the woman was brought forward, even though the man involved was equally guilty. Jesus didn't facilitate their unjust actions but instead challenged their motives, ultimately exposing their hypocrisy.

We need wisdom to know when and how to speak out, but when God nudges us to stand up for those who are less confident or unable to defend themselves, we should be ready to act. Our silence, like Pilate's, isn't neutral – it's a choice.

Reflections

As Christians, why is it important that we fight against injustice?

What examples in the Bible illustrate God's hatred of injustice?

Have you ever stayed silent in the face of wrongdoing? What stopped you from speaking up, and how might you respond differently next time?

Practical Task

This week, identify a small injustice you can address – whether it's supporting someone who's been unfairly treated or challenging a negative comment. Ask God for the courage to be a voice of truth and kindness in that situation.

....

....

The Crucifixion

"It is not the strength of the
body that counts, but the
strength of the spirit."
- J.R.R. Tolkien

68. Reading: Matthew 27:27-56

Sometimes, what's familiar to us can become so commonplace that we start to take it for granted. This is captured in the phrase, 'Familiarity breeds contempt.' When we become accustomed to something or someone we can lose the respect and value we once had for it or them. This is something we must guard against, especially when it comes to the sacrifice Jesus made on the Cross.

We've seen the crucifixion depicted in films, documentaries, and even cartoons, and perhaps over time, we've stopped feeling as moved as we once did. But the significance of what Jesus endured should never become ordinary to us. In this devotional, we're going to approach it from a fresh perspective. I invite you to read the account of the crucifixion and then write your own response to the incredible sacrifice Jesus made for you on the Cross.

Reflections

Choose one of the following questions to reflect on:

How does the reality of Jesus' suffering and sacrifice deepen your understanding of love and forgiveness?

In what ways might you have become desensitised to the significance of the crucifixion? How can you rekindle a deeper appreciation for this profound sacrifice?

How does the crucifixion shape your perspective on sin, redemption, and your daily walk with Christ?

God of the Detail

"Great things are not done by impulse, but by a series of small things brought together." - Vincent van Gogh

69. Reading: Matthew 27:57-60

The creation of the world is a powerful example of God's attention to detail. God can simultaneously see both the larger picture and the miniscule details that comprise it. This understanding should inspire confidence in us, knowing that God sees and cares about every aspect of our lives. The role Joseph of Arimathea played at the close of Jesus' earthly life is a profound illustration of this truth.

Here is what we know about Joseph. He was wealthy, and at some point, he encountered Jesus personally or heard His teachings and became a disciple. Joseph's bold request for the body of Jesus also suggests that he was probably at Jesus' crucifixion. It is worth considering the privilege Joseph had in using his resources to give Jesus a proper burial. Joseph's final act of service should lead us to reflect on what selfless acts of service we can offer to God.

It's interesting to note the symmetry in Jesus' life: His earthly father, who was present at His birth, was named Joseph. Then, as Jesus' life drew to a close, another Joseph, divinely appointed, played a crucial role. These two Josephs – likely strangers who never met – were instrumental in the pivotal moments of Jesus' life. This should fill us with confidence as we realise that God is intricately involved not just in the life of His Son but in our lives as well, as His adopted children.

Reflections

Reflect on times when you have seen God's hand in the details of your life. How did this awareness impact your faith?

Consider the role of Joseph of Arimathea. How can you, like Joseph, use your resources and position to serve God in a meaningful way?

Practical Task

Identify a practical way you can serve others selflessly, as Joseph did, and make a plan to act on it this week.

....
....
....
....
....
....
....
....
....
....
....
....
....
....

Our Great Commission

"Go into the world and do well. But more importantly, go into the world and do good." - Minor Myers Jr.

70. Reading: Matthew 28:16-20

Farewells are never easy, especially when parting from someone you deeply care about. As Jesus prepared to ascend into heaven, a beautiful exchange took place: God for God. The Son departed, and God the Holy Spirit descended to dwell within us. We were not left alone, nor were we short-changed by Jesus' departure.

The disciples, who had answered Jesus' call to follow Him, could not have imagined the path that lay ahead. In the days leading up to the ascension, they experienced an emotional whirlwind: fear as Jesus was seized in Gethsemane, shame as they fled, despair at Judas' betrayal, and grief at his suicide. They felt the deep sting of loss when Jesus died on the Cross. But now, on the mountain in Galilee, they meet with unimaginable joy as they encounter the risen Jesus, just as He promised. However, this meeting is bittersweet; Jesus is about to leave them once more, and this time, they won't see Him again in their lifetime.

When they next see Jesus, it will be as the victorious Saviour who will right every wrong and conquer sin once and for all.

But until then, Jesus gives them – and us – a clear directive: the Great Commission. This wasn't just a command for the 11 disciples; it's a commission for every believer. We are called to go into the world, make disciples, baptise them, and teach them to follow everything

Jesus has commanded. It's not a polite suggestion but a direct order – the final instruction Jesus gave before His ascension.

We must honestly examine whether we are living out this commission. If we're not engaged in making disciples, we need to ask ourselves why. It's the mission Jesus left us with until He returns.

Reflections

Why is the Great Commission not just a command for the original disciples but for all believers?

How can you actively participate in making disciples in your everyday life?

Are there fears or obstacles that have kept you from fully engaging in the Great Commission? How can you address them?

Practical Task

This week, take a step towards fulfilling the Great Commission. Whether it's sharing your faith with someone, encouraging a fellow believer, or offering to pray for someone in need, look for a practical way to make disciples and share the love of Jesus in your daily life.

....
....

Epilogue

I began this devotional with three aims. I hope they have been achieved. I pray that as you have waded through the waters of Matthew, you have questioned, been inspired, and—most of all—found your faith deepened.

The Gospel of Matthew is more than words on a page; it is an invitation. An invitation to wrestle with truth, to see Jesus through fresh eyes, and to step beyond the shallows into the depths of His wisdom and grace. If this journey has prompted you to think differently, read more deeply, or draw closer to God, then this book has served its purpose.

But the journey doesn't end here. Faith is not a destination but a lifelong pursuit. As you close these pages, I encourage you to keep going—keep asking, keep seeking, keep diving deeper. Return to Matthew, explore the other Gospels, and let Scripture continue to challenge and transform you.

Thank you for allowing me to be part of your journey. My prayer is that you never settle for the shallows but continue to wade into the limitless depths of God's truth, love, and grace.

Elle Louise James
February 2025

Acknowledgments

I could not have written a single word without the Holy Spirit.

Thank you! I am deeply introverted and would never have ventured to do something like this without Your leading – and sometimes dragging – me forward.

Thank you also to: Hayley, Claire, Debbie, Michaela and Alena – who have all supported and nudged me forward in different ways. Rachel, Rosel, Josh and Tasha for the quiet support.

A special thank you to Sara and Mon, who read each reading as I wrote it and forgave my mistakes. Pastor Lorraine, thank you for ensuring I remained theologically true to the text, and thanks also to Ashley, who polished my grammar. A final thank you to Rica, an angel on earth, who patiently supported me through endless design changes.

Above all, I am grateful to God who inspired this work and brought the right people into my life to make it possible.

www.ingramcontent.com/pod-product-compliance
Lightning Source LLC
Chambersburg PA
CBHW071110160426
43196CB00013B/2528